WALKS IN
LANCASHIRE WITCH COUNTRY

AN ILLUSTRATED GUIDE TO
THIRTY CIRCULAR WALKS
ON AND AROUND PENDLE HILL

JACK KEIGHLEY

MOUNT PLEASANT METHODIST CHAPEL | WALK 25

2

WALKS IN LANCASHIRE WITCH COUNTRY

an illustrated guide to
thirty circular walks
on and around Pendle Hill

by

Keighley

CICERONE

2 POLICE SQUARE, MILNTHORPE, CUMBRIA LA7 7PY
www.cicerone.co.uk

Second edition, reprinted 2008 and 2012
ISBN-13: 978 1 85284 446 2
ISBN-10: 1 85284 446 9

Also by *J Keighley*

WALKS IN THE YORKSHIRE DALES
ISBN 1 85284 034 X

WALKS IN THE YORKSHIRE DALES – BOOK TWO
ISBN 1 85284 065 X

WALKS IN THE YORKSHIRE DALES – BOOK THREE
ISBN 1 85284 085 4

WALKS ON THE NORTH YORK MOORS
ISBN 1 85284 134 6

WALKS ON THE NORTH YORK MOORS – BOOK TWO
ISBN 1 85284 197 4

FAMILY WALKS IN THE FOREST OF BOWLAND
ISBN 1 85284 251 2

WALKS IN RIBBLE COUNTRY
ISBN 1 85284 284 9

WALKS IN DALES COUNTRY
ISBN 1 85284 323 3

SOUTH PENNINE WALKS
ISBN 1 85284 390 X

INTRODUCTION

In 1612 ten 'Pendle Witches' went to the scaffold. These depraved wretches and their supposed victims lived in the villages and farmsteads surrounding Pendle Hill. Though nearly four centuries have since elapsed, the drama has never been forgotten, and the mere mention of Pendle is enough to evoke visions of witchery and black magic. The aura of witches so pervades the area that you can scarce travel a mile without thinking of them.

But there's more — much more — to Pendle than witches. For many folk the image of Lancashire is one of brash seaside resorts and dismal terraced streets in grimy mill towns, but the walker in Pendle will discover a Lancashire rich in natural beauty; a region which offers an exciting range of attractions varied enough to suit all conceivable tastes and interests : —

- ★ wild, windswept, gritstone moorlands, whose moods alter with every subtle change of light and shade
- ★ green and fertile valleys, with shady woodlands and exquisitely beautiful riverside walks
- ★ gently rolling farmland, with patchwork fields and flowery meadows
- ★ sparkling streams rushing and tumbling down deep, wooded cloughs
- ★ picturesque villages, historic buildings and hoary old farmsteads — each with a story to tell
- ★ extensive and panoramic views
- ★ relics of ancient civilizations
- ★ nature reserves, country parks and reservoirs
- ★ quiet leafy lanes, canal towpaths, ancient packhorse trails and a vast network of public footpaths

In the course of my exploratory wanderings I have met and talked with many farmers and local folk — good-natured people all, whose warm friendliness and kind help I have greatly appreciated.

In this modern life of bustle and stress there is no better form of escapism than a country walk. Whether you walk for bodily exercise, relaxation of the mind, or the enjoyment of natural scenery and places of interest, you will not be disappointed by what Pendle has to offer.

But enough of this. If you were born and bred in this area, as I was, you will love it and not need me to extol its virtues. If, on the other hand, you've not yet discovered Pendleside, then it's really time you did something about it. So get your boots on and give it a try — you'll be bewitched!

J Keighley
2004

THE PENDLE WAY

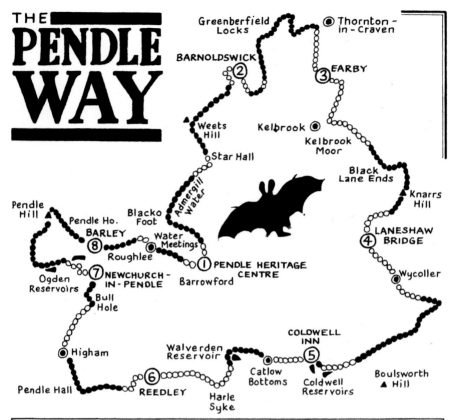

Sections of Pendle Way which coincide with walks in this book

The possibility of creating a long-distance walk in the area was first mooted in 1985. A working party was set up, headed by Pendle Borough Council and including Pendle Enterprise Trust, Pendle Heritage Centre and the Manpower Services Commission. Construction work, grant-aided by the Countryside Commission, began in July 1986, and the resultant 'Pendle Way' is a 45-mile circular walk around the Borough of Pendle, with waymarkers featuring a witch and yellow arrow. Those interested in walking this splendid route could not do better than purchase a set of informative leaflets 'The Pendle Way' (grant-aided by the Countryside Commission and written by Pendle Heritage Centre). These describe the route in clockwise direction, covering the walk in 8 sections. The starting-points of each section are shown on the map.

The Pendle Witches

The dramatic and complex story of the Pendle Witches unfolded during the spring and summer of the year 1612. It is a story which has left an indelible mark on the countryside around Pendle, which will be forever known as the 'Hill of the Witches'. Pendleside visitors will very soon become aware of the light-hearted sort of 'witch cult' which has developed in the area; there was nothing light-hearted, however, about the witch-hunt which led to the public hanging of ten wretched individuals — eight women and two men — at Lancaster on 20th.August 1612.

Who or what were these so-called Pendle Witches? Certainly they were *not* witches of the classic (black cloak, pointed hat, black cat, whizzing about on broomstick) tradition. In the main they were ignorant peasants — social outcasts — scraping a meagre living by begging and stealing. They probably believed — or half-believed - that they *were* witches, with special powers, and the drugs, such as belladonna and aconite, which they no doubt took may well have induced such delusions. They also knew that if they could convince the local populace of their power to kill or maim through witchcraft then they could use threats and blackmail to demand what they wanted from anyone they chose. In this respect they had the advantage of living in an age when there was a great deal of superstition, a general belief in witchcraft and an irrational fear of the supernatural.

In 1612 there were two notable families of 'witches' in the area — the Demdike Brood and the Chattox Clan, and their respective senior members were the two most feared local witches. Both would be about eighty at this time, and both were withered, decrepit, sightless old crones. Mother Demdike (real name Elizabeth Southernes) lived at Malkin Tower, where she brought up her children and grandchildren as practising witches. Her daughter, Elizabeth Device, was, besides being mentally depraved, an exceedingly ugly creature (she was nicknamed 'Squintin' Lizzie'). Also in residence at Malkin Tower were Lizzie's dim-witted son James, her wild and emotional daughter Alizon and a younger daughter, Jennet, who was only nine years old in 1612. Old Chattox lived in a hovel at Greenhead, near Fence. Her real name was Anne Whittle (the nickname 'Chattox' came from her maiden name of Chadwick). This repulsive old hag, who was given to ceaseless and incomprehensible prattle, had two daughters — Elizabeth (Bessie) Whittle and Anne Redfearne. There was bitter enmity between the two families, who terrorized each other as well as the rest of Pendle.

On the 18th. March 1612 Alizon Device set off for Trawden on a begging expedition. Near Colne she met one John Law, a Halifax pedlar, whom she asked for some pins. When the pedlar refused, Alizon began to curse him vehemently, and instructed a black dog, which had suddenly appeared on the scene, to attack him. Law collapsed, and was carried, paralysed and bereft of speech, into a nearby ale-house. His son, Abraham, was summoned from Halifax to investigate the incident, and as a result of his inquiries Alizon, James and Elizabeth Device were commanded to appear, on the 30th. March, before Roger Nowell Esq., Magistrate, of Read Hall.

Nowell was an expert in complex legal matters, and was a

skilled, if unscrupulous, interrogator. He also had a strong belief in, and fear of, witchcraft. Under pressure, Alizon not only confessed to being a witch, but also incriminated her grandmother, Demdike. The black dog at Colne, Alizon insisted, was her 'familiar' (No self-respecting witch would be without a 'familiar' — a demon or spirit, usually in animal form, attendant upon the witch and obeying her commands. The black cat is the classic 'familiar'). James gave evidence against his sister who, at the end of the proceedings, was detained in custody, whilst James and his mother were released.

Further dubious evidence found its way to Nowell, and on the 2nd. April Demdike, Chattox and Anne Redfearne were brought for interrogation to Ashlar House, Fence. Demdike confessed to witchcraft and denounced Chattox (who also confessed) and Anne. On the 4th. April all three of them, together with Alizon, were taken via Bowland to Lancaster Castle, there to await trial under the Witchcraft Act of 1604.

Six days later, on Good Friday, a Witches' Assembly and Feast was held at Malkin Tower. Among those present were Elizabeth, James and Jennet Device, Christopher Howgate (Demdike's son) and his wife, Alice Nutter of Roughlee, Jane Bulcock and her son John, of Moss End Farm, Newchurch, Katherine Hewet (known as 'Old Mouldheels') of Colne, Alice Grey, also of Colne and Jennet Preston of Gisburn. Alice Nutter was quite unlike the others in that she was a gentlewoman — well-educated and wealthy. Jennet Preston had just been acquitted at York Assizes on a charge of witchcraft.

When news of this Good Friday gathering reached the ears of Roger Nowell it was embroidered with some highly fanciful allegations. The witches, it was said, were planning to 'spring' their four colleagues from Lancaster Gaol and, furthermore, were plotting to blow up the Castle and murder the gaoler, Thomas Covell. Most of those who attended the Witches' Feast were rounded up for questioning, during the course of which James and Jennet Device gave damning evidence — some of it against their own family. James and his mother Elizabeth confessed to being involved in witchcraft, and all but one of the accused were bundled off to Lancaster to be tried at the August Assizes. The exception was Jennet Preston, the Gisburn witch. As Gisburn was then in Yorkshire she was sent for trial at York, where she was found guilty and hanged on the 29th. July.

On the 16th. August Sir Edward Bromley and Sir James Altham travelled from York to Lancaster to sit in judgement of nineteen indicted witches. The leading lady, however, didn't make it, for old Demdike had died in her cell. Roger Nowell was the Prosecutor, and Thomas Potts came from London to act as Clerk of Court. His copious records were to form the basis of a book 'The Wonderfull Discoverie of Witches in the Countie of Lancaster' which was published in 1613.

To say that the trial was one-sided would be an under-statement. The defendants had no professional representation, and most of the evidence offered would today have been totally unacceptable. In addition to this, the 'star' witness for the prosecution was the nine-year-old Jennet Device. So self-assured and word perfect was she that there seems little doubt that she had been carefully primed, coached and brain-washed.

8

Ten of the 'Pendle Witches' were found guilty, and nine of them – Old Chattox, Elizabeth, James and Alizon Device, Anne Redfearne, John and Jane Bulcock, Alice Nutter and Katherine Hewet – went to the gallows at Lancaster on the 20th. August 1612, together with one Isabel Robey of Widnes. Margaret Pearson, of Padiham, who was prosecuted by Nicholas Bannister, was sentenced to stand in the pillory (on market days) at Clitheroe, Whalley, Padiham and Lancaster before serving a one-year's term of imprisonment. Alice Grey was acquitted.

In 1633 there was a further outbreak of supposed witchcraft at Hoarstones, Fence. Seventeen (including Jennet Device) were sentenced to death, but reprieved by the King (Charles I).

Note : The names of the 'witches' in this account are as spelt by Potts in his records of the Lancashire Summer Assizes. In some cases the accuracy is open to doubt (e.g. 'Device' was very probably 'Davies')

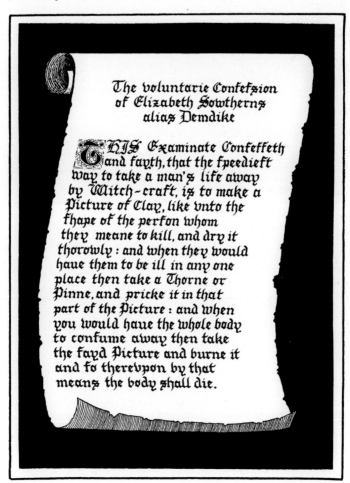

The voluntarie Confeßion of Elizabeth Sowtherns alias Demdike

THIS Examinate Confeßeth and fayth, that the fpeedieft way to take a man's life away by Witch-craft, iß to make a Picture of Clay, like vnto the fhape of the perfon whom they meane to kill, and dry it thorowly : and when they would haue them to be ill in any one place then take a Thorne or Pinne, and pricke it in that part of the Picture : and when you would haue the whole body to confume away then take the fayd Picture and burne it and fo therevpon by that meanß the body shall die.

PENDLE HILL

'Penighent, Pendle Hill, Ingleborough,
Three such hills be not all England through.
I long to climbe up Pendle ; Pendle stands
Rownd cop, survaiying all ye wilde moorelands.'

These words, written by the parson/poet Richard James during his 1636 tour of Lancashire, illustrate the impact which Pendle Hill had, and still has, on its beholders.

But why should this be so ? Pendle is not a great mountain ; in fact it is not a mountain at all, its summit failing by 169 feet to attain that distinction. In general appearance it rather resembles an upturned boat - plain and simple and somewhat dull. It lacks the rugged sort of profile displayed by the aforementioned Penyghent and Ingleborough, and has none of the bristling crags and soaring arêtes of the volcanic hills of Cumbria. In truth, Pendle Hill is a very ordinary, common or garden fell, so why should it be so famous ?

The answer lies in its geographical position, for Pendle stands in complete isolation between the main South Pennine Chain and the rolling Bowland Fells. Thus, having no competition, it rises majestically and appears much higher than it really is. It is instantly recognisable when viewed from any angle, and it dominates the surrounding countryside to a greater extent than does, perhaps, any other hill in the land.

What Pendle lacks in height it certainly makes up for in girth, for it is no less than seven miles in length and covers an area of about twenty-five square miles. The hill looks at its best when sun and clouds conspire to dapple its slopes with ever-changing patterns of light and shade, but it is a moody giant, and on a dull, cheerless day can appear sullen and sombre. Legends of witchcraft and black magic, strange superstitions and whispered tales of supernatural happenings have given Pendle an almost mystical atmosphere. Pass close to the hill on a wild, drab winter's day and you half-expect to catch sight of a black-cloaked, besom-mounted witch gliding silently by.

Pendle Hill has kept its size and shape because of its summit layer of hard, weather-resistant gritstone. The top of the hill is a vast, flat plateau of peat hags and coarse grasses. From the breezy summit the view must be one of the finest in England - a magnificent panorama of infinite variety and charm. Especially dramatic and beautiful is the prospect to the north-west across the Forest of Bowland towards Lancaster (where the Pendle witches languished and died) and the distant, hazy hills of Lakeland. Equally delightful is the northern aspect, looking along Ribblesdale to the 'Three Peaks' and Yorkshire's limestone country. To the north-east are the Craven Fells, whilst close-at-hand to the south and east lies a string of Lancashire industrial towns - Accrington, Padiham, Burnley, Brierfield, Nelson, Barrowford and Colne. Far away to the south-west, beyond the Mersey estuary, lie the mountains of Snowdonia, whilst finally, in the west, you may see the glint of the sun on the Irish Sea and even that much-sought landmark Blackpool Tower.

You will, of course, be very fortunate indeed to find yourself standing atop Pendle on a day clear enough for you to behold all these wonders.

Over the ages this brooding old hill has silently witnessed a whole pageant of human history. At the dawn of civilisation, when the valleys were heavily wooded and marshy, our early Bronze Age ancestors made their homes on Pendle's upper slopes. To this wild country came the Brigantes — a hardy and warlike Iron Age race — and the Romans, who established an important military centre at nearby Ribchester. The Normans constructed a castle on a limestone knoll at Clitheroe, and by the 13th C. clearings (booths) were being cut in the forests and small cattle farms (vaccaries) were being set up. The great cavalcade of history flowed on through Pendle's shadows ; the Wars of the Roses, the Civil War and the witches came in turn, left their mark and were gone. In those far-off days Pendle was a link in a chain of beacons, and many a bonfire has blazed on its summit in times of trouble or celebration. One of the biggest was lit in June 1887, when over a thousand loyal subjects gathered on Pendle to celebrate Queen Victoria's Jubilee. Generations of mill-workers, seeking respite from the grimy streets of nearby cotton towns, found recreation and rural pleasure on the slopes of Pendle, and thus pioneered the pastime of hill-walking which today has so very many adherents.

The affection with which local people have regarded dear old Pendle throughout history is nowhere better expressed than in the words of Nicholas Assheton in Harrison Ainsworth's classic novel 'The Lancashire Witches' : -
'I love Pendle Hill, and from whatever side I view it — whether from this place (Whalley Nab), where I see it from end to end, from its lowest point to its highest, from Padiham, where it frowns upon me, from Clitheroe, where it smiles, or from Downham, where it rises in full majesty before me - from all points and under all aspects, whether robed in mist or radiant with sunshine. Born beneath its giant shadow, I look upon it with filial regard. Its broad, round, smooth mass is better than the roughest, craggiest, shaggiest, most sharply-splintered mountain of them all. And then what a view it commands! There is no hill in England like Pendle Hill!'

PENDLE HERITAGE CENTRE

PARK HILL, BARROWFORD, NELSON, BB9 6JQ. TEL (01282) 661701

Park Hill is the former home of the Bannister family, of which the most famous member is Dr. Roger, the 4-minute miler. The Bannisters first settled here c 1450, but the oldest surviving parts of the house are 16th C. A continuing programme of restoration has preserved these buildings and converted them to house exhibitions about the history of the Pendle area. There is a video and exhibition about the infamous witches, a 15th C. style cruck barn and a re-created 18th C. walled garden. The shop has a multitude of books on local history, architecture, gardening and walking, plus masses of souvenirs and gifts. The Tea Room offers a wide range of temptations. The Centre also houses the Pendle Arts Gallery and the Tourist Information Centre.
OPEN DAILY (except Christmas Day) 10-5.

Nestling at the foot of Pendle Hill in Newchurch in Pendle, this wonderfully creepy shop sells spooky souvenirs and an array of books on the fact and fiction of witchcraft and the fascinating story of the Pendle Witches. This is THE place to go for memorabilia, model witches, maps, posters, T-shirts, pottery, pictures, postcards, walking guidebooks, cassettes, CDs etc., etc. WITCHES GALORE is open daily 11-5 (Wed 1·30-5). Closed Christmas Day and Boxing Day.   Tel : (01282) 613111

ABOUT THIS BOOK

THE WALKS All the walks described in this book are circular, and begin at a place where a car may be parked without causing an obstruction. They are fairly uniform in length, an average of about 6 miles making them half-day rather than full-day excursions. Though not every location visited has a known direct link with 'witchcraft', all the walks have starting points within 8 miles (as the broomstick flies) of the summit of Pendle Hill, and thus lie exclusively in that small corner of Lancashire where local 'witchlore' prevails. The routes, which adhere to public rights-of-way and permissive paths, should be free from serious difficulty and well within the capability of reasonably fit and agile walkers. Although the author has personally researched and walked all these routes, it must be pointed out that changes will occur quite frequently. Walkers may expect to encounter new stiles and fences and even diversions – either temporary or permanent. In such cases please note and obey all legitimate waymarks and signs.

NEITHER THE AUTHOR NOR THE PUBLISHER CAN ACCEPT RESPONSIBILITY FOR ANY ACCIDENT OR MISADVENTURE INCURRED ON THESE WALKS.

THE MAPS The strip-maps show all relevant route-finding features, and great care has been taken to ensure accuracy, although for the sake of clarity there is deliberate distortion of scale in depicting routes along, for example, narrow lanes or through farmyards. In all maps north is at the top. In the Route Directions any mention of a stile, gate or footbridge means that it is used, unless otherwise stated. The maps and route directions together should suffice to make it quite clear to you how you've got lost. Nevertheless, it is strongly recommended that an Ordnance Survey map be carried, as this will add interest and enable the walker to identify distant features not mentioned in the text. All the walks are covered by three O.S. EXPLORER (1:25 000) MAPS, viz :-

Explorer 19 West Pennine Moors
Explorer OL 21 South Pennines
Explorer OL 41 Forest of Bowland and Ribblesdale

WALKING IN WITCH COUNTRY

★ Many of the routes in this book cross agricultural land, and farmers will not welcome inconsiderate visitors. When crossing fields keep closely to paths and walk in single file across meadows. Avoid climbing walls, and securely close all gates behind you (unless they are obviously meant to be left open).

★ Cars must not be parked where they obstruct field gates or cause damage to grass verges. Lock your car securely and hide from view any attractive or valuable items (or take them with you).

★ Some of the routes described in this book cross high, exposed moorland terrain where the weather conditions can change very quickly. It should not be assumed that, because it's a nice warm day at valley level, it will necessarily be so at, say, the summit of Pendle. Should the weather turn nasty, don't hesitate to call it a day and return by the route along which you came.

★ Before setting out, let others know exactly where you're going (especially if you're walking alone).

★ When walking along a motor-road walk on the RIGHT to face oncoming traffic. The exception to this is on the approach to a blind right-hand bend, when you should cross to the left for a clearer view.

CLOTHING AND EQUIPMENT

Boots or strong, comfortable shoes are essential (on the high moors and in winter BOOTS are the ONLY suitable footwear). A windproof jacket (preferably with a hood) will be needed. Thick, heavy sweaters are not a good idea — two or three lightweight layers are warmer and more adaptable to changing conditions. Denim is not at all suitable. In cold weather a woollen hat or cap will prevent the loss of a great deal of body heat. A rucksack is necessary. A small 'day-sack' with a capacity of about 20-25 litres would be adequate for any of these walks. The author's rucksack will always contain the following items :-

● waterproof jacket and overtrousers ● small first aid kit ● spare laces ● large scale O.S. map ● compass ● whistle ● plastic bottle for cold drink and/or flask for coffee or soup ● a high-calorie snack (e.g. chocolate or crisps) ● dog's drinking-water in a plastic bottle with either a 'cup-top' or a separate small bowl

In wet, muddy conditions gaiters are an asset, once you've managed to get them on (it helps if you're a contortionist). A walking-stick is a matter of personal preference. Some walkers wouldn't be seen dead with one, but the author finds a knobstick useful for steep, slippery descents, fording streams, beating down nettles, discouraging aggressive animals and testing potentially boggy ground prior to sinking in up to the knees.

14

The best knobsticks are made from hazel, apple or ash. Folding, or telescopic, metal jobs which are stuffable into a rucksack are now popular (though a bit pricey).

CHILDREN

When taking children on country walks some thought must be given to distance and the type of terrain involved. Until you're sure of the child's capabilities, keep the distance short. Most of the walks in this book would probably be too much for a child under the age of five. As a rough rule-of-thumb, a child should be able to manage about a mile for each year of his age after his fifth birthday. Children should be warmly clothed and well-shod. One cannot always afford to buy expensive boots for growing feet, but at least the child should have strong shoes or close-fitting wellies. On no account should young children be allowed to wander off beyond the range of vision of responsible adults, and extreme care and control must be exercised in the vicinity of crags, quarries, canals, old mine workings and ruined buildings.

DOGS

Though dogs are generally better-behaved than children they can nevertheless present certain difficulties which the owner should bear in mind. The two main problems are livestock and stiles — particularly ladder-stiles. Dogs should be kept under close control at all times, and MUST be on a lead in the proximity of farmyards and farm livestock. You will be lucky to complete any of these walks without meeting cattle and/or sheep. A lead should also be used when walking on motor-roads or on moorland during nesting time (April – June). Some large, agile dogs are able to scramble over ladder-stiles, but small models need to be lifted over, and this can sometimes be rather awkward if you're walking alone. If your dog is big, fat and rheumaticky then you have problems. Best places for dogs are high, open ground and woodland; worst are motor-roads and lowland pastures. On very hot, sunny days dogs can become distressed, and may be at risk of heat-stroke. On summer walks the author has in his rucksack a small, plastic spray-bottle of water.

THE WALKS

№		MILES
1	THE HEART OF WITCH COUNTRY	7¼
2	DOWNHAM AND TWISTON	5
3	OVER SPENCE MOOR	6½
4	THE VALE OF WYCOLLER	6
5	PENDLE HILL FROM NICK O' PENDLE	6¾
6	THREE RIVERS WALK	6¾
7	BOWLAND BYWAYS	7
8	WALVERDEN RESERVOIR	6¼
9	NOGGARTH RIDGE AND NEWCHURCH	4½
10	WEETS HILL	6
11	PENDLETON AND WORSTON	5¼
12	THE LOST VALLEY OF THE TREACLE MINES	5¼
13	LIMESTONE LANDSCAPES	4½
14	BEACON HILL	6½
15	PENDLE HILL FROM BARLEY	5
16	GREAT EDGE AND NOYNA ROCKS	6
17	WADDINGTON	6
18	THE LEAFY LANES OF RIMINGTON	5½
19	A CANALSIDE WALK IN CRAVEN	5
20	WISWELL AND NICK O' PENDLE	5¾
21	ROUGHLEE AND THE WATER MEETINGS	5¾
22	A VISIT TO BRACEWELL	6½
23	PENDLE HILL FROM DOWNHAM	6
24	READ HEIGHTS	6¼
25	WHITE MOOR AND ADMERGILL WATER	7¼
26	WHALLEY AND THE NAB	5¾
27	BOULSWORTH HILL	6½
28	KELBROOK MOOR	7
29	AROUND STANG TOP	4¾
30	PAYTHORNE AND GISBURNE PARK	5¾

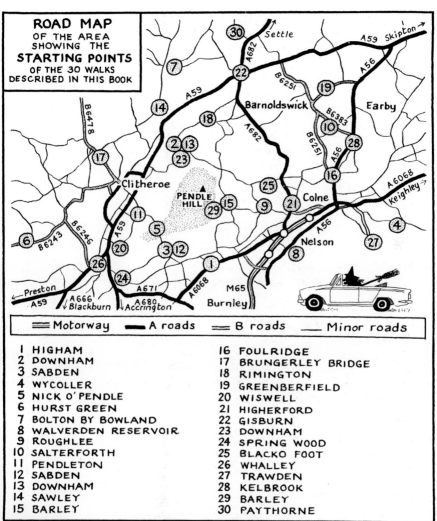

ROAD MAP
OF THE AREA
SHOWING THE
STARTING POINTS
OF THE 30 WALKS
DESCRIBED IN THIS BOOK

Motorway — **A roads** — **B roads** — **Minor roads**

1 HIGHAM	16 FOULRIDGE
2 DOWNHAM	17 BRUNGERLEY BRIDGE
3 SABDEN	18 RIMINGTON
4 WYCOLLER	19 GREENBERFIELD
5 NICK O'PENDLE	20 WISWELL
6 HURST GREEN	21 HIGHERFORD
7 BOLTON BY BOWLAND	22 GISBURN
8 WALVERDEN RESERVOIR	23 DOWNHAM
9 ROUGHLEE	24 SPRING WOOD
10 SALTERFORTH	25 BLACKO FOOT
11 PENDLETON	26 WHALLEY
12 SABDEN	27 TRAWDEN
13 DOWNHAM	28 KELBROOK
14 SAWLEY	29 BARLEY
15 BARLEY	30 PAYTHORNE

 INFORMATION CENTRES

PENDLE HERITAGE CENTRE Park Hill, Barrowford, Nelson, Lancs BB9 6JQ. Tel:(01282)661701.

CLITHEROE TOURIST INFORMATION CENTRE 12-14 Market Place, Clitheroe, Lancs BB7 2DA. Tel: (01200) 425566.

BARNOLDSWICK TOURIST INFORMATION CENTRE Post Office Buildings, Fernlea Avenue, Barnoldswick, Lancs BB18 5DL. Tel: (01282) 666704.

SYMBOLS USED ON THE MAPS

✠ church with tower ♠ church with spire

+ church or chapel without either

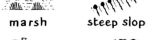

buildings

crags

woods, forests

lakes, reservoirs

marsh

steep slope

boulders, outcrops

quarries

BS boundary stone

MS milestone

GP guidepost

MP marker post

▲ △ cairns

Route (not necessarily a visible path)

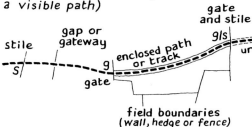

stile

gap or gateway

enclosed path or track

gate

gate and stile

unfenced road

cattle grid

cart track

motor road

field boundaries
(wall, hedge or fence)

★

THE BEST PLACES ON THE WALK (IN THE AUTHOR'S OPINION)

waterfall

FB

footbridge

river

ravine

stream

direction of flow

ABBREVIATIONS
USED IN THE TEXT

R right   L left   RH right-hand   LH left-hand   FP footpath
BW bridleway   SP signpost   wm waymarked   PW Pendle Way

PLEASE OBSERVE THE
COUNTRY CODE

- Enjoy the countryside and respect its life and work
- Use gates and stiles to cross walls and fences
- Keep your dog under close control
- Protect wildlife, plants and trees
- Help to keep all water clean
- Make no unnecessary noise
- Fasten all gates

Leave livestock, crops and machinery alone ●

Keep to public paths across farmland ●

Take special care on country roads ●

Guard against all risk of fire ●

Leave no litter ●

LITTER

THE HEART OF WITCH COUNTRY

7¼ MILES

P Higham. At extreme East end of village, adjacent to main A6068, is short section of obsolete road. Cars and broomsticks can be parked here.

Grid ref: 813 367

ROUTE DIRECTIONS ① ▶ Walk into village. Just past church turn L (FP sign) along enclosed path. Go L along main road for 60 yds to stile on R. ② ▶ Bear slightly L across field to stile. Go R down tarmac lane and keep straight on down fields. ③ ▶ Just before footbridge take stile on L. Walk parallel with river to stile near river bend. Straight on through trees (clear path). ④ ▶ When farm appears aim well to L of it, to a marker-post. Cross footbridge and follow LH field boundary. Cross footbridge and turn R to cross motorway. Turn L across field to stile and steps. ⑤ ▶ Go L up road. Turn R into drive of Newlaund Farm. Pass L of farm and forward along track. ⑥ ▶ Turn R past far end of cottages then drop L to footbridge. Cross stile (hidden behind hawthorn) and climb slightly R to gate.

Through stile to cross small lawn, go L along drive and R down road. ⑦ ▶ Just before reaching motorway fork L. At bottom of hill turn L (FP sign) along rough lane. Keep L at fork and go straight on past Old Laund Hall. ⑧ ▶ When track ends take stile on L and follow RH hedge. Cross road to enclosed path. At top of field go R over stile then L past cottages. ⑨ ▶ Turn L along road.

cont. on next page

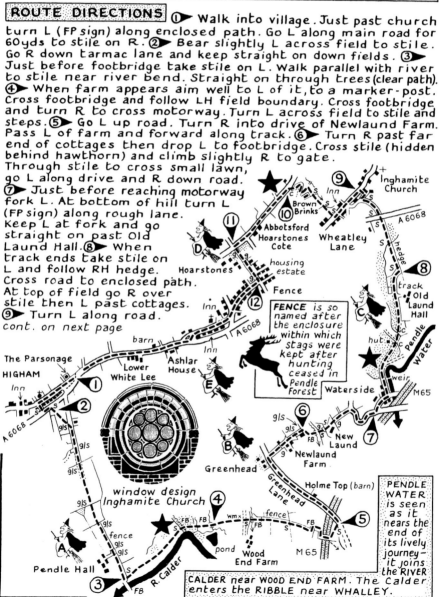

FENCE is so named after the enclosure within which stags were kept after hunting ceased in Pendle Forest

window design Inghamite Church

PENDLE WATER is seen as it nears the end of its lively journey — it joins the RIVER

CALDER near WOOD END FARM. The Calder enters the RIBBLE near WHALLEY.

20

Scenically the least attractive walk in the book, but given pride-of-place because of its many connections with the Pendle Witches. From HIGHAM, where dwelt the ghastly CHATTOX and several of her 'victims', the undulating route takes in GREENHEAD (scene of the witches' earliest foul deeds), HOARSTONES (alleged haunt of witches in 1633) and ASHLAR HOUSE (where witches were interrogated prior to being despatched to LANCASTER and the gallows). No ladder-stiles. 2½ miles on motor-roads, but the busier ones all have walkways.

ROUTE DIRECTIONS cont : Take stile on R opposite 'Laund View' (bungalow). Pass R of big house, climb to third powerline pole, turn L across field then R up drive. ⑩ Go L along road. ⑪ Turn L through iron kissing-gate. Descend to join housing-estate road. When it turns L go straight on down 'snicket' at corner. ⑫ Turn R along Wheatley Lane Road, bear L at junction then R along continuation of Wheatley Lane Road. Turn R along main road.

HIGHAM is partly industrialised but has some very attractive old cottages. The Four Alls Inn displays an unusual sign and has an interesting old horse-trough.

PENDLE HALL is Victorian but is built 17th C. style and incorporates several features of the much older house which it replaced. CHATTOX, one of the most infamous witches, and her daughter, ANNE REDFEARNE, are thought to have lived near here, in a squalid hovel close to the river.

GREENHEAD

At the Lancaster Witch Trials of 1612, Chattox and Anne Redfearne were found guilty of causing by witchcraft the deaths of, respectively, Robert Nutter and his father Christopher. Robert and Christopher, of Greenhead, had, on their deathbeds some 18 years previously, claimed to have been bewitched. Greenhead is one of the finest houses in Pendle, but cannot, unfortunately, be well-seen from the road.

The **INGHAMITE CHURCH** was the first to be built (1750) by followers of the Rev. Benjamin Ingham (a colleague of John Wesley), and is the second oldest place of worship in Pendle Forest. It was rebuilt in 1897.

OLD LAUND HALL was the home of the Robinsons, who were involved as witnesses in the 'Hoarstones' witch trials.

ASHLAR HOUSE

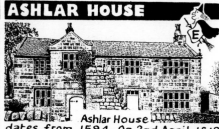

HOARSTONES

In 1633 a coven of 'witches' began to meet at the then uninhabited house, led by JENNET DEVICE who, as a young child, had given evidence against her own family. A boy claimed that he was held prisoner by the 'witches' on Hallowe'en 1633. He named 17 of his captors and trials were held in 1634. Some were gaoled, and 4 were sent to London to be shown to huge crowds.

Ashlar House dates from 1594. On 2nd April 1612 Demdike, Chattox and Anne Redfearne were interrogated here and sent for trial. On 27th April Elizabeth, James and Jennet Device were also brought here for questioning.

MAP O.S. Explorer OL 21 South Pennines

DOWNHAM & TWISTON

5 MILES

P Downham. Car park and toilets at lower end of village, near the bridge. Grid ref: 784 441

Everything at Downham is beautiful – even the toilets. Uniquely designed and spotlessly maintained, they're worth looking at even if you don't want to go.

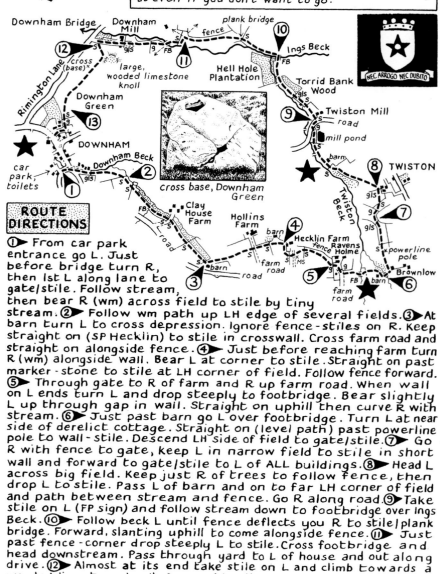

Downham Bridge Downham Mill plank bridge
fence
⑫ /cross (base)ˣ
Rimington Lane
large, wooded limestone knoll
⑪ Hell Hole Plantation ⑩ Ings Beck
NEC ARROGO NEC DUBITO
Downham Green
⑬
Torrid Bank Wood
DOWNHAM
Twiston Mill road
mill pond
⑨
car park, toilets ① Downham Beck ② barn ⑧ TWISTON
cross base, Downham Green ⑦
Twiston Beck
ROUTE DIRECTIONS
Clay House Farm Hollins Farm barn ④ Hecklin Farm Ravens Holme
fence powerline pole
③ farm road ⑤ FB barn Brownlow
farm road

① From car park entrance go L. Just before bridge turn R, then 1st L along lane to gate/stile. Follow stream, then bear R (wm) across field to stile by tiny stream. ② Follow wm path up LH edge of several fields. ③ At barn turn L to cross depression. Ignore fence-stiles on R. Keep straight on (SP Hecklin) to stile in crosswall. Cross farm road and straight on alongside fence. ④ Just before reaching farm turn R (wm) alongside wall. Bear L at corner to stile. Straight on past marker-stone to stile at LH corner of field. Follow fence forward. ⑤ Through gate to R of farm and R up farm road. When wall on L ends turn L and drop steeply to footbridge. Bear slightly L up through gap in wall. Straight on uphill then curve R with stream. ⑥ Just past barn go L over footbridge. Turn L at near side of derelict cottage. Straight on (level path) past powerline pole to wall-stile. Descend LH side of field to gate/stile. ⑦ Go R with fence to gate, keep L in narrow field to stile in short wall and forward to gate/stile to L of ALL buildings. ⑧ Head L across big field. Keep just R of trees to follow fence, then drop L to stile. Pass L of barn and on to far LH corner of field and path between stream and fence. Go R along road. ⑨ Take stile on L (FP sign) and follow stream down to footbridge over Ings Beck. ⑩ Follow beck L until fence deflects you R to stile/plank bridge. Forward, slanting uphill to come alongside fence. ⑪ Just past fence-corner drop steeply L to stile. Cross footbridge and head downstream. Pass through yard to L of house and out along drive. ⑫ Almost at its end take stile on L and climb towards a wooded limestone knoll. On reaching it veer R and head for upper end of distant wood. ⑬ Go L alongside wood. On passing through a small gate turn R along tarmac drive to emerge into village at pub.

Undulating and fairly easy, the only strenuous bit being the final climb over DOWNHAM GREEN. No ladder-stiles, but dog-walkers may find some of the wall-stiles a little awkward. Motor-road walking negligible. If you only ever do one walk from this book, make sure it's this one. You may scour the length and breadth of ENGLAND, but you won't find a prettier walk. *Grander, maybe, or more spectacular, but not prettier.* Walk it slowly and savour it, for this is truly Arcadia.

★ DOWNHAM ★

Assheton Arms

This picture-postcard village is one of the loveliest in Lancashire. DOWNHAM HALL, at the N end of the village, has been the family seat of the ASSHETONS (armorial shield and motto depicted on previous page) since 1558. The Elizabethan mansion was extensively rebuilt in 1835 in classic Georgian style. The beautiful ST. LEONARD'S CHURCH was built as recently as 1909-10 (except for the tower, which is 15th C.) to replace a very plain building erected after the 15th C. church was pulled down in 1800. There has been a church here, however, since at least 1283, and probably long before that - possibly even in Saxon times. OLD WELL HALL, at the lower end of the village near the bridge, is a superb Tudor house, whilst grouped around the green are typical 18th and 19th C. HANDLOOM WEAVERS' COTTAGES. Downham and the Assheton family feature prominently in Harrison Ainsworth's famous novel 'THE LANCASHIRE WITCHES'. In 1961 the village was used as the location for 'WHISTLE DOWN THE WIND', a highly acclaimed film starring Hayley Mills. More recently Downham was the setting for the BBC TV series 'BORN AND BRED'.

derelict cottage, point ⑥

TWISTON is a scattered community of grey stone cottages and ancient farmsteads. The name was recorded c1140 as 'Twyssulton', and opinion is divided as to whether this means 'a place where streams meet' or 'a town on a boundary'. The latter seems likely, for Ings Beck, until 1974, divided Lancashire and Yorkshire, and, ages ago, formed part of the boundary between the Saxon kingdoms of Mercia and Northumbria. ●

TWISTON MILL was originally a corn mill, but converted to a cotton mill in the early 19th C. In its peak production years the mill employed 20 men, 7 women and 22 children. The children were 'cotton piecers'; this was a dangerous job entailing working under the machinery, and serious accidents were common. The mill closed after a fire in 1882.

Twiston Mill

| MAP | O.S. Explorer OL 21 South Pennines OR O.S. Explorer OL 41 Forest of Bowland and Ribblesdale. |

OVER SPENCE MOOR

6½ MILES

P Sabden. Car park and toilets opposite the White Hart Inn.
Grid ref: 779 374

ROUTE DIRECTIONS

①▶ Turn R past White Hart then first L. ②▶ Turn R along lane (with seats at end of it). Continue along farm road. ③▶ Fork L towards farm. Just before yard take swing-gate (wm) on R. Follow wall (ignore step-stile in it) to gate/stile. Cross field to gate/stile in crosswall and on towards building. ④▶ Pass L of derelict farm and keep just L of fence/hedge to stile (wm). Bear L to stile (hidden by gorse) then head for house. ⑤▶ Cross footbridge, through gate L of house, then turn R behind house to gate (wm). Go forward along valley then bear L up to gate/stile in front of big house (Sabden Old Hall). Go L up road and L at junction. ⑥▶ Turn R past near side of houses and up through stiles to climb alongside wooded clough. ⑦▶ From gate/stile at top turn L to climb along RH side of gully to gate-stile. Straight on (WNW) up boggy moor to ladder-stile in crosswall. Bear slightly L to locate a clear path to another ladder-stile. Turn R to follow wall on R. ⑧▶ At a ladder-stile in this wall DON'T CROSS IT but turn sharp L along clear path. Keep L at fork. At boulder-strewn hollow turn R. Skirt rim of hollow to locate clear path dropping towards reservoir. Cross stream just above plantation and follow track to reach motor-road at a cattle-grid. ⑨▶ Go R up road and L (BW sign) along farm road. ⑩▶ 50yds past a barn turn L (wm) and drop to gate/stile in LH corner. Follow tiny stream down, keeping L of wall to gate/stile. Descend to RH end of buildings. ⑪▶ Turn L through metal gate and forward through gate/stile. Go R down tarmac lane. When it bends R go L over step-stile by gate, then turn R to follow fence/hedge. Turn R down road to Sabden.

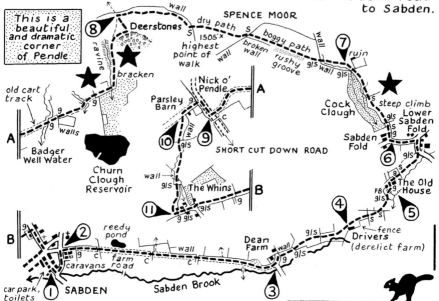

This is a beautiful and dramatic corner of Pendle

SPENCE MOOR

Deerstones

dry path

⑧

ravine

bracken

1505' x highest point of walk

broken wall

boggy path

rushy groove

wall

ruin

⑦

Nick o' Pendle

A

Cock Clough

steep climb

Lower Sabden Fold

old cart track

walls

Parsley Barn

⑩

⑨

SHORT CUT DOWN ROAD

Sabden Fold

⑥

A

Badger Well Water

Churn Clough Reservoir

wall

The Whins

B

The Old House

F8

④

⑤

fence

Drivers (derelict farm)

⑪

reedy pond

②

B

caravans farm road

Dean Farm

⑨

car park, toilets ① SABDEN

Sabden Brook

③

Looming sombrely over the SABDEN VALLEY is the sprawling hump of SPENCE MOOR, and a walk over this southern flank of PENDLE HILL will appeal to lovers of bleak and desolate places. But there is sylvan beauty too, notably in the vicinities of COCK CLOUGH, CHURN CLOUGH RESERVOIR and THE WHINS. Quite strenuous, with about 1000' of ascent, including a stiff climb alongside COCK CLOUGH, and some rough, boggy terrain on the moor. 2 ladder-stiles. Less than ½ mile on motor-roads.

 SPENCE MOOR IS DANGEROUS IN MIST

SABDEN, a village with no pretensions to beauty, lies at the foot of the steep road which leads over the Nick o' Pendle to Clitheroe. The village was industrialised by cotton manufacturer Richard Cobden in the 1820s. Cobden, a philanthropist who encouraged his employees to read, established a school and library in the village. The oldest part of Sabden is Heyhouses, to the north-east, which dates from the 16th C. There are three churches - Parish

White Hart Inn, Sabden

Church (built 1846), Baptist Church (1910) and R.C.Church. The latter was built in the 1930s with stone from a demolished mill at Rochdale, at a total cost of £800. For some reason Sabden has always been the butt of local humour (for notes on 'treacle mining' see Walk 12).

Dean Farm

This hoary old farmhouse was built in 1574, which makes it one of the oldest houses in the area. Above the lower set of mullioned windows is a lengthy and much-eroded inscription. The house has associations with the Lancashire Witch Trials of 1612.

SABDEN OLD HALL

has been extensively rebuilt, but parts of the house date from the 16th and 17th centuries.

The derelict farmhouse of DRIVERS. Above the door is a datestone 1792.

DEERSTONES is a huge, boulder-strewn hollow- an impressive place.

The 16-acre CHURN CLOUGH RESERVOIR is a fly fishery stocked with trout.

PARSLEY BARN may take its name from John PASLEW, the last Abbot of Whalley Abbey, who was executed in 1537 (see Walk 20).

MAPS O.S. Explorer 19 West Pennine Moors AND O.S. Explorer OL 21 South Pennines.

THE VALE OF WYCOLLER

4

6 MILES

P Wycoller. The Country Park has two car parks — Haworth Road and Trawden Lane. Use the latter, reaching it by leaving the A6068 at either Colne or Laneshaw Bridge.

Grid ref : 927 395

Note : Motor-cars, save for those of residents, essential services and disabled badge holders, are not allowed to progress beyond the car park.

ROUTE DIRECTIONS

① From car park go R down walkway, then lane, into village. ② At far end of village go between Aisled Barn and toilets to path slanting L uphill. It soon turns R to go through wide gateway. ③ In 200yds take gate/stile (wm) on R. Cross field to stile (wm) and path on LH side of fence. Path forks twice (wm) – each time keep L uphill. Climb around wall-corner to ladder-stile. ④ Straight on to cross farm road and up to top of rocks. Pass wall-corner just beyond and keep straight on with wall on L. ⑤ At foot of steep descent go L over wall-stile (wm) then turn L (wm) to climb back up again! Follow wire fence to paved path (wm) into pub car park. Go R along road for a good half-mile. ⑥ Turn sharp R down to gate and cart-track. ⑦ In half-a-mile fork R off main track (FP Wycoller, Pendle Way) and follow wall to gate. Continue ahead, keeping fairly close to wall on L. Path eventually goes L through gate and drops to stream. ⑧ Ford stream, scramble up bank and at top turn R to gate/stile at wall-corner. Path gradually descends to stile close to stream. Cross next field and at its far end turn L and climb steep hillside to gate in wire fence near outcrops (View Point Rocks). ⑨ Turn R through gateway (wm) and stay parallel with wall on R to stile in crosswall (NOT the corner-stile on the R). ⑩ Turn L to crumbling wall and walk along its RH side. Keep straight on through two stiles and a gate, then follow a rushy ditch to a path between walls. ⑪ At its end take small gate on R and follow ditch towards farm. At end of ditch turn R and head for derelict farm, via two wall-stiles. Go through gate into yard and L along access road. ⑫ At crosstracks (by gate) turn R and head for conifers. Path descends through edge of wood to lane down to Wycoller.

HAWORTH ROAD can be quite busy. TAKE CARE

on a fine day, a great place to eat your smoked salmon butties

WYCOLLER, one of PENDLE'S best-loved beauty spots, is a fascinating place. Here, where witch territory merges with Brontë country, you don't just see history – you *feel* it. This undulating and moderately strenuous walk is mostly on well-waymarked tracks and paths. Just over half-a-mile on a motor-road. One ladder-stile. Safe in mist.

WARNING The ford at point ⑧ may be a problem if the stream's in spate after rain.

WYCOLLER, an ancient village rescued from seemingly inevitable dereliction, is one of Lancashire's prettiest and most romantic places. During the 17th and 18th centuries Wycoller became a thriving handloom weaving centre, but fell into decline when the invention of power looms took the textile industry to town mills. In the 1890s a proposal was made to create a reservoir by damming the beck near the aisled barn, but luckily the scheme was never implemented. In 1950 a society called 'Friends of Wycoller' was formed and began some restoration work on the then deserted and crumbling village. Despite this the chances of Wycoller's survival looked slim until, in 1973, renovation and maintenance were assured when Lancashire County Council bought the estate. **THINGS TO SEE** : PACK-HORSE BRIDGE (illustrated) Possibly 13th C. CLAPPER BRIDGE Probably late 18th C. PIERSON'S HOUSE (illustrated) Named after family who lived here in 18th C. HALL Thought to be 'Ferndean Manor' of Charlotte Brontë's 'Jane Eyre'. Built in 16th C. Extended 1744. Abandoned 1818. AISLED BARN Superb structure built 1630s. CLAM BRIDGE Short detour upstream from Aisled Barn. Single slab bridge, one of oldest in England. The village has a well-stocked GIFT SHOP/TEAROOM.

VACCARY WALLING Upright stone slabs erected to enclose a 'vaccary' (monastic cattle farm). The examples seen on this walk were probably built in the 13th C.

FOSTER'S LEAP TWO HUGE BOULDERS, SEPARATED BY A 6' GAP, NAMED AFTER ONE FOSTER CUNLIFFE WHO JUMPED SAFELY (SO IT IS SAID) FROM ONE TO THE OTHER

COOMBE HILL CROSS Reached by a sunken path (not a right-of-way) rising from a gate opposite Coombe Hill Cross Farm. Of uncertain origin, but obviously of great antiquity.

The Herders Inn

This lonely inn stands by the Haworth Road. Once called the Oldham Arms, it has been a pub since 1860, but existed long before that.

MAP   O.S. Explorer OL 21 South Pennines

PENDLE HILL
FROM NICK O' PENDLE

6¾ MILES

P Nick o' Pendle, on the Sabden – Clitheroe road. Park in the old quarries at the highest point of the road, 500yds S of the Wellsprings Inn.

Grid ref: 772 385

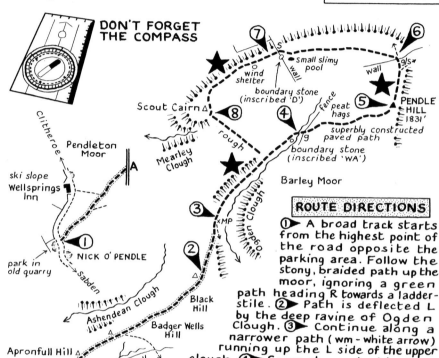

DON'T FORGET THE COMPASS

Small slimy pool
wind shelter
boundary stone (inscribed 'D')
Scout Cairn △
peat hags
wall
7
6
8
4
5
PENDLE HILL 1831'
superbly constructed paved path
rough
Mearley Clough
boundary stone (inscribed 'WA')
Barley Moor

Clitheroe
Pendleton Moor
ski slope
Wellsprings Inn
park in old quarry
NICK O' PENDLE **1**
Sabden
Ashendean Clough
Black Hill **2**
Badger Wells Hill
Apronfull Hill △
wall
3
×MP
Ogden Clough

ROUTE DIRECTIONS

① A broad track starts from the highest point of the road opposite the parking area. Follow the stony, braided path up the moor, ignoring a green path heading R towards a ladder-stile. **②** Path is deflected L by the deep ravine of Ogden Clough. **③** Continue along a narrower path (wm - white arrow) running up the L side of the upper clough. **④** Cross stream to kissing-gate in fence. Broad, rising path soon becomes paved. When pavings end, the summit O.S. column is in view directly ahead. **⑤** Turn L (N) at summit and head for gate/ladder-stile in wall. **⑥** Cross the ladder-stile (gate won't open) and go L along clear path to reach another ladder-stile. **⑦** Head for circular stone wind-shelter (expertly and sturdily built). Follow sketchy path along the edge of the escarpment to a large, beehive-shaped cairn (Scout Cairn). **⑧** Turn ½ L (set compass SE 130°) across rough, tussocky moorland. There's no path, so proceed with care and beware hidden bogholes. Rejoin the outward route in Ogden Clough and turn R to retrace your steps to Nick o' Pendle. (Should you wish to visit Wellsprings Inn look out, near the end of the walk, for a path descending R to that establishment).

At the summit of Pendle Hill

With a starting point at 1000' and no steep climbing, this is by far the easiest route to the top of PENDLE. It's a grand walk, but not, however, one to be considered in bad weather conditions, for the entire journey lies across wild, windswept moorland totally exposed to the elements. A compass MUST be carried, and should be used at SCOUT CAIRN to determine one's course across a pathless expanse of rough moor. 2 ladder-stiles. No motor-roads.

APRONFULL HILL

is the highest point of Pendleton Moor, and an old local legend attempts to explain how it came by its unusual name. Apparently it was here that a rather nasty giant took a huge boulder from his apron and hurled it at Clitheroe Castle, knocking a gaping hole in the castle wall. The strain of perpetrating this mindless act of vandalism caused his apron strings to snap, spilling out the remaining boulders to form a ring of stones on the ground which remains there to this day.

NICK O' PENDLE is a favourite haunt of hang-gliders.

Wheatear ♂

As you tramp these bleak hillsides, look out for the WHEATEAR, a summer visitor easily recognised by its conspicuous white rump displayed in flight. The handsome male has prominent black cheek-stripes.

TWO BOUNDARY STONES SEEN ON THE WALK

WA — Point ④   D — Point ⑦

BENCH MARK

An Ordnance Survey sign. It marks a spot where the height above sea-level has been accurately measured. The horizontal line above the arrowhead marks the exact altitude. When a surveyor takes other altitude measurements from the bench mark he fixes an angle-iron at the level of the horizontal line as a temporary bracket to support his instruments

— •-●-• —

THE MOST EXHILARATING SECTION OF THE WALK IS THAT BETWEEN POINTS ⑦ AND ⑧. FROM THE RIM OF PENDLE'S STEEP NORTHERN DECLIVITY THERE IS A STUNNING VIEW ACROSS THE RIBBLE VALLEY TO THE BEAUTIFUL BOWLAND FELLS (THOUGH IT HAS TO BE CONCEDED THAT THE CEMENT WORKS IS A MONSTROUS BLOT ON THE LANDSCAPE).

Wellsprings Inn

SCOUT CAIRN

is a prominent Ribble Valley landmark, and 3 memorial tablets built into the splendidly constructed 10' high monument explain its name.

Keep Fido on a lead during the nesting season (April-June).

| MAP | O.S. Explorer OL 41 Forest of Bowland and Ribblesdale. |

THREE RIVERS WALK

6¾ MILES

P Hurst Green. Parking space in the village is rather limited. The best place to leave the car would be a small layby ¼ mile E of the village along the Whalley road. Grid ref: 691 382

ROUTE DIRECTIONS

① Walk into village. Go down LH end of Shireburn Arms to gate/stile. Descend field, keeping R (wm) of tiny stream. ② Cross two footbridges then bear L. Cross stile and go L to path down through woodland. Cross footbridge and follow riverside path. ③ Join farm track and follow it up-stream (DON'T go L into farmyard). ④ Pass R of house (Boat House) and straight on to riverbank path, which soon becomes a farm track. ⑤ At farm go L (RW sign) through gate. At farmhouse turn R through yard. Pass pond and go straight on up main track. ⑥ Take kissing-gate (wm) on R. Cross fields to come alongside wood on R. When it ends maintain direction through line of stiles. ⑦ Go R along road. At near end of bridge go L (FP sign) to follow farm track alongside river. Keep straight on at Trout Cottage. ⑧ Cross stone bridge and turn L along track with stream on L. Go L over footbridge to climb steep wooden steps, then bear R along top edge of wood. Cross stile and turn R to follow edge of wood. Through gate/stile and forward along farm road. ⑨ Go R along road for just under ½ mile. Take entrance to College (FP sign). Pass College and church and keep straight on. ⑩ Where tarmac road bends L take gate (wm) on R. Keep to RH edge of fields. At second kissing-gate turn L along LH side of fence/hedge. Follow track past school to main road. Turn L.

✳

The noble Jacobean mansion seen across the river at point ④ is **HACKING HALL** (built 1607)

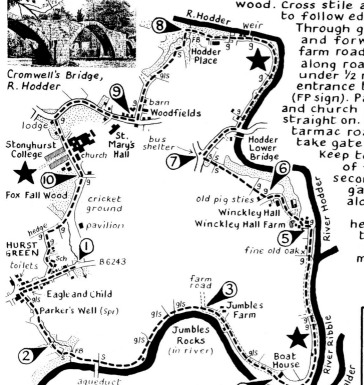

Cromwell's Bridge, R. Hodder

R. Hodder
weir
⑧
FB
Hodder Place
9ls
barn
Woodfields
⑨
lodge
Stonyhurst College
St. Mary's Hall
church Hall
bus shelter
⑦
s/s
Hodder Lower Bridge
⑥
River Hodder
⑩
Fox Fall Wood
cricket ground
pavilion
old pig sties
Winckley Hall
Winckley Hall Farm
⑤
fine old oak
hedge
HURST GREEN
toilets
Sch
①
B6243
Eagle and Child
Parker's Well (Spr)
farm road
③
Jumbles Farm
Jumbles Rocks (in river)
②
FB
aqueduct
River Ribble
River Calder
River Ribble
Boat House
④

30

A lovelier riverside walk can scarce be imagined, for here, where the HODDER and CALDER flow into and swell the RIBBLE, is some of the most beautiful countryside in LANCASHIRE. The walk's outstanding highlights are a superb old packhorse bridge and a magnificent college in a glorious parkland setting. Very easy-going; the only strenuous bit is the steep flight of steps (132 of the perishers) above point ⑧. 1 small ladder-stile (with an adjacent gate. 1 mile on motor-roads (mostly with walkways).

HURST GREEN

is not a particularly pretty village, but it contains much of interest and is well-loved by Lancashire ramblers. The Shireburn Arms is named after the family which owned Stonyhurst. It was on roads around Hurst Green in 1826 that John L. McAdam first tried out his construction methods.

The walk offers an opportunity to observe a wide variety of waterside birds. Look out especially for the CORMORANT, which, though primarily a bird of the coast and estuary, sometimes travels a fair way inland along river valleys.

THE HACKING FERRY

A ferry once operated across the Ribble near its confluence with the Calder, but was discontinued in 1954.

Cormorant

The boatman's house was, at the time of writing (Aug 03), being rebuilt. The illustration shows how it looked in 1991. An old ferry boat, found in a barn in 1983, was restored and can be seen in Clitheroe Castle Museum.

The L-shaped pond at **WINCKLEY HALL FARM** is the remains of a moat.

THE GRACEFUL ARCHES OF THE OLD LOWER HODDER BRIDGE HAVE SPANNED THE HODDER SINCE 1562. CROMWELL IS SAID TO HAVE MARCHED HIS TROOPS OVER IT EN ROUTE FOR THE BATTLE OF PRESTON IN 1648, BUT THIS SEEMS UNLIKELY. IT IS, HOWEVER, KNOWN LOCALLY AS 'CROMWELL'S BRIDGE'. THE NEW ROAD BRIDGE WAS BUILT BY JOHN McADAM IN 1826.

STONYHURST

West Front and Church

This former Elizabethan mansion was begun in 1592 by Sir Richard Shireburn, the local landowner. After the death of the last Shireburn - Sir Nicholas - in 1717, the house fell into disrepair, and in 1794 was handed over to the Society of Jesuits. Since then it has been extended and developed to become one of the country's most eminent public schools. The college museum houses some priceless relics of Renaissance times, and the library has some very rare books, including the oldest existing English bound book — a 7th C. copy of St. John's Gospel. The magnificent W. front is flanked by the beautiful St. Peter's Church, built 1832-5. Famous ex-pupils include Sir Arthur Conan Doyle and the actor Charles Laughton.

MAP	O.S. Explorer 19 West Pennine Moors.

QUANT IE PUIS

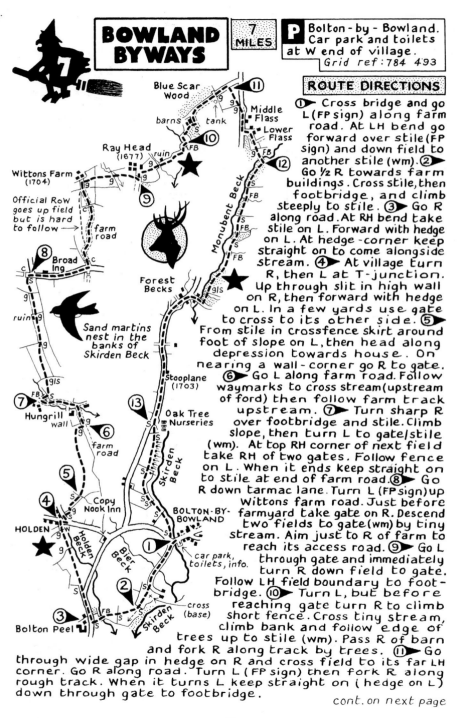

BOWLAND BYWAYS

7 MILES

P Bolton - by - Bowland. Car park and toilets at W end of village.
Grid ref : 784 493

ROUTE DIRECTIONS

① Cross bridge and go L(FP sign) along farm road. At LH bend go forward over stile (FP sign) and down field to another stile (wm). ② Go ½ R towards farm buildings. Cross stile, then footbridge, and climb steeply to stile. ③ Go R along road. At RH bend take stile on L. Forward with hedge on L. At hedge-corner keep straight on to come alongside stream. ④ At village turn R, then L at T-junction. Up through slit in high wall on R, then forward with hedge on L. In a few yards use gate to cross to its other side. ⑤ From stile in crossfence skirt around foot of slope on L, then head along depression towards house. On nearing a wall-corner go R to gate. ⑥ Go L along farm road. Follow waymarks to cross stream (upstream of ford) then follow farm track upstream. ⑦ Turn sharp R over footbridge and stile. Climb slope, then turn L to gate/stile (wm). At top RH corner of next field take RH of two gates. Follow fence on L. When it ends keep straight on to stile at end of farm road.⑧ Go R down tarmac lane. Turn L (FP sign) up Wittons farm road. Just before farmyard take gate on R. Descend two fields to gate (wm) by tiny stream. Aim just to R of farm to reach its access road. ⑨ Go L through gate and immediately turn R down field to gate. Follow LH field boundary to footbridge. ⑩ Turn L, but before reaching gate turn R to climb short fence. Cross tiny stream, climb bank and follow edge of trees up to stile (wm). Pass R of barn and fork R along track by trees. ⑪ Go through wide gap in hedge on R and cross field to its far LH corner. Go R along road. Turn L (FP sign) then fork R along rough track. When it turns L keep straight on (hedge on L) down through gate to footbridge.

cont. on next page

Map labels

Blue Scar Wood
Middle Flass
Lower Flass
barns
tank
Ray Head (1677)
ruin
FB
Wittons Farm (1704)
Official Row goes up field but is hard to follow →
farm road
Broad Ing
Forest Becks
ruin
Sand martins nest in the banks of Skirden Beck
Monubent Beck
Stooplane (1703)
Oak Tree Nurseries
Hungrill
wall
farm road
Skirden Beck
BOLTON-BY-BOWLAND
Copy Nook Inn
HOLDEN
Holden Beck
Bier Beck
car park, toilets, info.
cross (base)
Bolton Peel
Skirden Beck

Walkers may catch a glimpse of the deer which roam this unspoilt countryside where the RIBBLE VALLEY merges with the verdant foothills of the magnificent FOREST OF BOWLAND. This gently undulating ramble, from the idyllic village of BOLTON-BY-BOWLAND, passes a succession of splendid 17th C. farmsteads. The path alongside MONUBENT BECK is rough underfoot in places and may be a bit overgrown. No ladder-stiles. Just under a mile on motor-roads.

ROUTE DIRECTIONS cont: ⑫▶ Follow beck downstream (white waymarks). Turn R along farm road then L along road. ⑬▶ At nurseries take stile (FP sign) on L. Forward to another stile, then follow beck down to Bolton-by-Bowland. Path keeps high above beck, not descending to water's edge until last field.

BOLTON BY BOWLAND

This is one of the region's prettiest villages. Listed in the Domesday Book, it was granted a market charter by Edward III in 1354, and a market was held here until the turn of the 20th C. The PARISH CHURCH is an absolute gem and must not be missed. It dates back at least to the 13th C., but was extensively rebuilt c 1464 by Sir Ralph Pudsay, whose tomb is quite remarkable. Fashioned in black limestone, it depicts Sir Ralph, his three (consecutive!) wives and his twenty-five children. Each wife has, in the folds of her dress, a numeral indicating the number of children she bore to Sir Ralph – Matilda 2, Margaret 6 and Edwina 17. Several pews bear the date 1694 and the initials of their first owners. The studded oak door is dated 1705 and the font is early 16th C. KEYS COTTAGE, one of the many quaint cottages along the main street, is dated 1716 and is so named because of the unusual design on its door-head. The VILLAGE GREEN has stocks and a medieval cross. The COACH AND HORSES is a most convivial 13th C. inn.

Cross base near point ②

BOLTON PEEL is a sturdy 17th C. farmhouse by which stands a fine preaching cross set in an ancient base. From the Peel family of Bolton Peel came Sir Robert (Prime Minister 1834-5, 1841-6). As Home Secretary he founded the modern police force (the term 'bobby' is derived from his name).

The waterfall just below the pretty hamlet of HOLDEN can look quite impressive when in spate. Make a short detour L at point ④ to view the splendid Broxup House (1687).

The path by MONUBENT BECK is a permissive one made available through the Countryside Stewardship Scheme, which offers financial assistance to landowners who are willing to help in conserving our countryside, its wildlife and historic features. At Monubent Beck the aim is to encourage a variety of flowers and grasses to recolonise the area.

Stooplane

Forest of Bowland

MAP O.S. Explorer OL 41 Forest of Bowland and Ribblesdale.

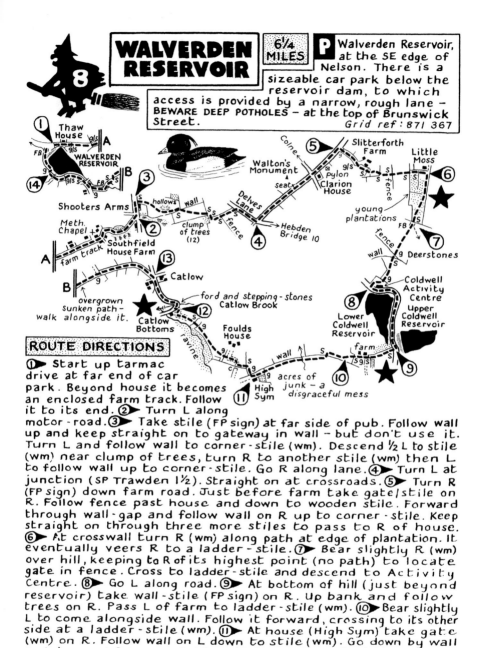

WALVERDEN RESERVOIR

6¼ MILES

P Walverden Reservoir, at the SE edge of Nelson. There is a sizeable car park below the reservoir dam, to which access is provided by a narrow, rough lane – BEWARE DEEP POTHOLES – at the top of Brunswick Street.
Grid ref: 871 367

8

Thaw House
FB
WALVERDEN RESERVOIR
Shooters Arms
Meth. Chapel
Southfield House Farm
hollows wall
clump of trees (12)
Delves Lane
Walton's Monument
seat
Colne
Slitterforth Farm
Little Moss
Pylon
Clarion House
young plantations
Deerstones
Hebden Bridge 10
Catlow
ford and stepping-stones
Catlow Brook
overgrown sunken path – walk alongside it.
Catlow Bottoms
Foulds House
ravine
High Sym
acres of junk – a disgraceful mess
Lower Coldwell Reservoir
Upper Coldwell Reservoir
Coldwell Activity Centre
farm
wall

ROUTE DIRECTIONS

① Start up tarmac drive at far end of car park. Beyond house it becomes an enclosed farm track. Follow it to its end. **②** Turn L along motor-road. **③** Take stile (FP sign) at far side of pub. Follow wall up and keep straight on to gateway in wall – but don't use it. Turn L and follow wall to corner-stile (wm). Descend ½ L to stile (wm) near clump of trees, turn R to another stile (wm) then L to follow wall up to corner-stile. Go R along lane. **④** Turn L at junction (SP Trawden 1½). Straight on at crossroads. **⑤** Turn R (FP sign) down farm road. Just before farm take gate/stile on R. Follow fence past house and down to wooden stile. Forward through wall-gap and follow wall on R up to corner-stile. Keep straight on through three more stiles to pass to R of house. **⑥** At crosswall turn R (wm) along path at edge of plantation. It eventually veers R to a ladder-stile. **⑦** Bear slightly R (wm) over hill, keeping to R of its highest point (no path) to locate gate in fence. Cross to ladder-stile and descend to Activity Centre. **⑧** Go L along road. **⑨** At bottom of hill (just beyond reservoir) take wall-stile (FP sign) on R. Up bank and follow trees on R. Pass L of farm to ladder-stile (wm). **⑩** Bear slightly L to come alongside wall. Follow it forward, crossing to its other side at a ladder-stile (wm). **⑪** At house (High Sym) take gate (wm) on R. Follow wall on L down to stile (wm). Go down by wall and descend farm road. When it turns R go straight on through gate. Descend to R of wooded ravine to locate cart-track down to road. **⑫** Go R across ford and up lane. **⑬** At 30 mph signs slow down and go L along walled track (FP sign). When wall on R ends keep straight on downhill. Cross stile on L and descend to footbridge. Follow path R and go R along farm road. When it

cont. on next page

Rural charm and solitude at the very edge of EAST LANCASHIRE'S industrial sprawl. The walk begins but a stone's throw from NELSON'S dreary terraced streets, and offers a wide variety of scenery ranging from the exposed uplands around COLDWELL to the sheltered, leafy glades of CATLOW BOTTOMS. Especially beautiful on a clear, frosty winter's day after a fall of snow. Undulating terrain. 3 ladder-stiles. 1¼ miles on quiet motor-roads. There's a smashing little café halfway round.

ROUTE DIRECTIONS cont: bends L cross wall-corner stile and follow wallside path. ⑭► Take metal gate on R to finish along lakeside path.

WALVERDEN RESERVOIR was built in 1869 to supply water to Nelson. It is designated as a Countryside Recreation and Wildlife Conservation Area. Many bird species flourish here, particularly in the reedy shallows at the head of the lake. A very popular coarse fishing venue.

The tiny hamlet of **SOUTHFIELD** has changed but little since the 18th C. John Wesley preached here on 18th April 1786, following which William Sagar converted his barn into a Methodist chapel - dated 1797 and still in regular use.

John Wesley 1703-91
Founder of Methodism

CLARION HOUSE

HAD ITS HEYDAY IN THE EARLY YEARS OF THE 20TH C. WHEN THE INDEPENDENT LABOUR PARTY LAUNCHED ITS WEEKLY NEWSPAPER 'THE CLARION' IN 1891, CIRCULATION WAS BOOSTED BY THE FORMING OF CYCLING CLUBS THROUGHOUT THE COUNTRY. CLARION HOUSES, BUILT BY VOLUNTEERS, PROVIDED REFRESHMENTS FOR CYCLISTS. BY THE END OF THE CENTURY THE HOUSE WAS IN A VERY DILAPIDATED STATE (as shown in the illustration), BUT IT HAS RECENTLY BEEN EXTENSIVELY RENOVATED.

LOWER COLDWELL RESERVOIR was completed in 1884 and holds 80 million gallons. The UPPER RESERVOIR, half the size, was opened in 1935.

WALTON'S SPIRE, atop an ancient stone shaft, was placed here by the Reverend Richard Wroe-Walton, of Marsden Hall, in 1835. Blown down by gales in 1984, it was re-erected and an information panel was sited beside it.

The Coldwell Inn had been a roadside pub for 100 years when it closed in 1939. During the 1920s it was a notorious den for illegal drinking and gambling – 52 people were arrested at a raid in 1922. An Activities Centre since 1989, the present building bears no resemblance to the original.

COLDWELL INN

| MAP | O.S. Explorer OL 21 South Pennines. |

NOGGARTH RIDGE & NEWCHURCH

4½ MILES | **P**

Roughlee. From the centre of the village drive along the Barley road. In a little less than ½ mile you will come to a roadside parking space on the river bank (at the end of some white railings). Park at right-angles to the road. *Grid ref : 839 399*

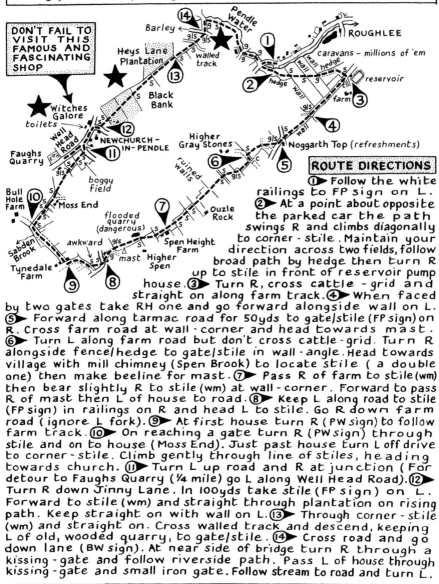

DON'T FAIL TO VISIT THIS FAMOUS AND FASCINATING SHOP

Barley ← / Heys Lane Plantation / Pendle Water / ROUGHLEE / caravans - millions of 'em / walled track / hedge / wall hedge / reservoir / Black Bank / farm / Witches Galore / toilets / NEWCHURCH-IN-PENDLE / Higher Gray Stones / Noggarth Top (refreshments) / Faughs Quarry / Wall Head Road / ruined walls / boggy field / Bull Hole Farm / Moss End / flooded quarry (dangerous) / Ouzle Rock / Sabden Brook / awkward / Spen Height Farm / Tynedale Farm / mast Higher Spen

ROUTE DIRECTIONS

① Follow the white railings to FP sign on L. **②** At a point about opposite the parked car the path swings R and climbs diagonally to corner - stile. Maintain your direction across two fields, follow broad path by hedge then turn R up to stile in front of reservoir pump house. **③** Turn R, cross cattle - grid and straight on along farm track. **④** When faced by two gates take RH one and go forward alongside wall on L. **⑤** Forward along tarmac road for 50yds to gate/stile (FP sign) on R. Cross farm road at wall - corner and head towards mast. **⑥** Turn L along farm road but don't cross cattle - grid. Turn R alongside fence/hedge to gate/stile in wall - angle. Head towards village with mill chimney (Spen Brook) to locate stile (a double one) then make beeline for mast. **⑦** Pass R of farm to stile (wm) then bear slightly R to stile (wm) at wall - corner. Forward to pass R of mast then L of house to road. **⑧** Keep L along road to stile (FP sign) in railings on R and head L to stile. Go R down farm road (ignore L fork). **⑨** At first house turn R (PW sign) to follow farm track. **⑩** On reaching a gate turn R (PW sign) through stile and on to house (Moss End). Just past house turn L off drive to corner - stile. Climb gently through line of stiles, heading towards church. **⑪** Turn L up road and R at junction (For detour to Faughs Quarry (¼ mile) go L along Well Head Road). **⑫** Turn R down Jinny Lane. In 100yds take stile (FP sign) on L. Forward to stile (wm) and straight through plantation on rising path. Keep straight on with wall on L. **⑬** Through corner - stile (wm) and straight on. Cross walled track and descend, keeping L of old, wooded quarry to gate/stile. **⑭** Cross road and go down lane (BW sign). At near side of bridge turn R through a kissing - gate and follow riverside path. Pass L of house through kissing - gate and small iron gate. Follow stream to road and turn L.

Of all the villages hereabouts, NEWCHURCH-IN-PENDLE is the most closely associated with tales of witchcraft. Our route of approach lies along the low, grassy ridge of NOGGARTH, which provides easy (if sometimes muddy) walking and grand sweeping views. The return to ROUGHLEE is by way of some of the loveliest scenery in Pendleside, ending with a riverside walk of exquisite charm. Lots of stiles; none are ladder-stiles, but there's an awkward sort of semi-ladder-stile just before TYNEDALE. To avoid it, stay on the road at point ⑧ and go R down the farm road. ⅓ mile on motor-roads.

NOGGARTH TOP is shown as Noggarth Cottage on the O.S. map. Refreshments are available here.

THE MYSTERY OF MALKIN TOWER*

MALKIN TOWER was the home of the Demdike Brood and the 'general HQ' of the 'witches' in the area. It has long since disappeared; it was probably a broken-down hovel in 1612, and may have been destroyed after the Witch Trials of that year. No one really knows exactly where the house was sited, but some historians believe that it stood between BULL HOLE and MOSS END.

These two farms both feature in the Pendle Witch story. At Bull Hole Demdike is said to have killed a sick cow after beeing paid by the farmer to cure it. Moss End was the home of mother and son Jane and John Bulcock, both hanged as witches in 1612.

* sounds like the title of an Enid Blyton 'Famous Five' story!

This face is carved on a rock in FAUGHS QUARRY. It is thought to be a memorial to a quarryman killed here in an accident around the turn of the 19th C.

NEWCHURCH-IN-PENDLE

The old houses of this quaint little village, many of them tall and whitewashed, are seemingly perched precariously on a steep hillside. A chapel-of-ease was established here c 1529, but the present church was built in the 18th C, after which the village, hitherto called Goldshaw Booth, adopted the name of 'Newchurch'. In the tower's west wall is a strange symbol known as the 'Eye of God' – a carved stone containing some oval glass. Near the porch the family grave of the Nutters is called the 'Witch's Grave', for Alice Nutter is reputedly interred here. Another 'witch' – Chattox – was alleged to have desecrated graves in the churchyard to collect skulls and teeth for use in casting evil spells.

'Witch's Grave'

Newchurch

MAP | O.S. Explorer OL 21 South Pennines **OR** O.S. Explorer OL 41 Forest of Bowland and Ribblesdale.

WEETS HILL

10

6 MILES

P Salterforth Bridge, just off the B6383 Kelbrook – Barnoldswick road. Small canalside car park almost opposite the Anchor Inn. *Grid ref: 887 453*

ROUTE DIRECTIONS

①► Start along towpath (canal on L). Just before bridge go up to road, cross bridge and take gate/stile on L (FP sign). ②► Bear R up field, aiming for small wood on skyline. Over fence-stile and cross next field to stile at its far LH corner. Turn R up through gap – stile and pass R of wall-corner to gate/ladder stile. ③► Straight on to come alongside crumbling wall on L. Cross it at a gap-stile (PW sign) and forward through small parking area to gravel track and lane. ④► Go R along road and fork L down Gillians Lane. ⑤► Turn L into Moorgate Road, which soon becomes a rough lane, climbing steeply through a big S-bend. ⑥► Just beyond Standridge Farm take gate/stile on R (PW sign). Climb alongside wall on L. ⑦► After passing head of ravine on R look out for a thin path forking R past a small cairn and on to the summit (O.S. column). Turn L and follow clear path to gate near house. Go forward along tarmac lane. ⑧► At second house on L take gate on L and up farm track. Through gate (wm), turn L to another gate (wm), then turn R to follow wall. Soon a clear path veers slightly L. Follow it to gate/stile at wall-corner. ⑨► Head for head! Pass through yard and on down access road. ⑩►Turn L down rough lane (concrete initially). ⑪► Turn R along road. ⑫► At last house on L (Knowlden House) take gate/stile (FP sign). Keep R of double fence then descend to gate/stile (wm) behind small mound. Head towards barn; there's a wall-stile 70 yds to its R. ⑬► Descend with wall on L, over gate/stile in crosswall and bear L to pass through stiles to L of tiny building. Cross next field to gate/stile. ⑭► Go R along farm road then L along lane.

Bancroft Mill (museum)

Letcliff Park

③

farm B6383

Park Bridge

toilets

s

Weavers Cottage

g/s

Standridge Farm

④ ⑪

②

canal

①

Anchor Inn

⑤

⑥ g/s

g/s

g/s

Lister Well Road (rough lane)

⑫

g/s g/s barn

g/s

fence

s wall

⑬

⑭

broken wall

wall s wall

ravine

fence

heather

★ seat
x
WEETS HILL 1250'

wall

⑦

Prospect Farm

Duck Pond

c c c c g

heather g

⑩

🍺

△ mast

Weets House

heather

tip

g/s

g g g

⑨ The stile at point ⑨ is a bit awkward, and the adjacent gate will probably be padlocked.

Gisburn Old Road

Sandyford

Lower Sandyford

⑧ Star Hall (an austere building)

☆ **FOR** ☆
A SHORTER ALTERNATIVE WALK
you could omit the Salterforth section by parking the car at Letcliff Park, which is signposted from the B6251 Colne – Barnoldswick road. Start at point ④ and turn L at point ⑪.   (4½ miles)

WEETS HILL is the easternmost bulwark of the PENDLE gritstone mass, for its tawny slopes sweep down into the light-green pastures of the WEST CRAVEN limestone country. Though of modest height, the summit is one of the finest viewpoints in PENDLESIDE. The walk is fairly strenuous, with a long climb of over 700' from MOORGATE ROAD to the summit. 1 ladder-stile. ½ mile on motor-roads.

British Waterways

The opening of the LEEDS – LIVERPOOL CANAL in 1816 brought prosperity to places like Barnoldswick, as the textile industry moved into mills.

BANCROFT MILL

was the last cotton-weaving shed built in Barnoldswick, in 1922. It closed in 1978 and was largely demolished, leaving only the chimney and engine house. The latter houses one of the few remaining mill steam engines still in working condition, a 600 hp job built at Nelson in 1915, and is open to the public during summer, with occasional 'steamings'.

WEETS HILL

IS ONE OF THE 'PENDLE THREE PEAKS', THOUGH AT 1250' IT IS VERY MUCH THE JUNIOR PARTNER. THE OTHERS ARE PENDLE HILL (1831') AND BOULSWORTH HILL (1696'). ON A CLEAR DAY THERE ARE BEAUTIFUL VIEWS OF THE MORE FAMOUS THREE PEAKS OF THE DALES.

The monstrous heads were fashioned in the 1980s by Peter Huby, art teacher and resident of Duck Pond

The bizarre statues of Duck Pond Farm

Lower Sandyford

WEETS HOUSE is named 'Stoops House' on old Ordnance Survey maps.

☆

GISBURN OLD ROAD was originally a busy packhorse route.

☆

The **ANCHOR INN** is one of Salterforth's oldest buildings, dating back to 1665, and is full of atmosphere and history. When the canal was built, the Travellers Rest, as the inn was then called, was below the water-line, so a new building was erected on top of the old one and re-named 'Canal Tavern'. Water seeping from the canal into the inn's limestone foundations has caused the growth of stalactites and stalagmites in the cellar.

MAP O.S. Explorer OL 21 South Pennines **OR** O.S. Explorer OL 41 Forest of Bowland and Ribblesdale.

PENDLETON & WORSTON

5¼ MILES

P Pendleton. Plenty of roadside parking spaces in the village. Be sure not to obstruct gates/drives or cause inconvenience to residents. The walk is described as starting from The Swan With Two Necks.   Grid ref : 755 396

ROUTE DIRECTIONS

①▶ Walk downstream to cart-track (FP sign) and gate/stile. Follow fence on R. Take metal gate on R and cross field to stile by powerline pole. Drop to far LH corner of next field (footbridge) and on to stile in A59 fence. **②▶** Go R alongside fence for 70 yds then cross A59 to gate/stile. Go ½ R to cross footbridge and straight on to gate/stile. Turn R along road and keep straight ahead at crossroads. **③▶** Beyond mast look out for gate/stile on R. IGNORE IT, but take NEXT STILE on R. Cross A59 to stile (wm). **④▶** Head L across field to metal gate. Go ½ R past a solitary ash and keep L of tall hedge to gate (BW sign). Go straight on to cross farm road (via gates). **⑤▶** Head for far LH corner of field. Cross stile and follow stream down to footbridge. **⑥▶** Straight on past powerline pole to stile, forward with fence to stile in hedge, then down to gate/stile at far LH corner. **⑦▶** Turn R along lane and go R at junction to follow road through village. **⑧▶** When road bends L turn sharp R (FP sign) and pass between buildings to gate/stile. Follow wall on L, then straight on up middle of field. Cross stile and make for far RH corner of next field (gated stile). **⑨▶** Follow fence on R up to farm road and turn R. **⑩▶** When farm road turns L (to Little Mearley Hall) keep straight on along rough track. It becomes a green track and then, at Lane Side, a farm road. Keep straight on along it for almost a mile. **⑪▶** Cross road and follow tarmac lane back to Pendleton.

WORSTON   Hall (site of)

sculpture   g/s   **⑧**

⑦   The Meadows   s by tree stump

⑥   s   FB   **⑨**   s with iron gate   fence

⑤   s   green track   c19

⑩   Little Mearley Hall

FP←   s   9   farm road

FP↙   **④**   tall hedge   FP←   Lane Side   ★

③   mast △   A59 Clitheroe Bypass   Mearley Hall

tarmac road   g/s   FB   g/s   farm road

②   c

farm   Pendleton Hall road

Howcroft Brook   **⑪**

g/s   g/s   **①**

★ PENDLETON   All Saints' Church

Where friends meet!

Calf's Head Hotel sign, Worston

The easiest walk in the book, with the only uphill section, between points ⑧ and ⑩, amounting to no more than about 150'. All the rest is level walking, mostly along leafy and floriferous lanes and farm roads linking two of the RIBBLE VALLEY'S prettiest villages. Sylvan scenery, with PENDLE'S ravine - gashed western slopes forming an impressive backdrop. No ladder-stiles. Just under a mile on quiet motor-roads.

☠ THE WALK INVOLVES TWO DEATH - DEFYING CROSSINGS OF THE RACETRACK KNOWN AS THE CLITHEROE BYPASS.

Pendleton

Though less well - known than places such as Waddington and Downham, this is one of the prettiest and best-kept villages in the area. A lively little brook (Swardean Beck) chuckles its way alongside the main street, watched over from either side by delightful 17th and 18th C. cottages. At the heart of the village is the curiously named 'Swan With Two Necks' — a pub which doubles as a Post Office. The church, which we shall pass almost at the end of the walk, was built in 1848. Pendleton was recorded (as 'Peniltune') in the 1086 Domesday Survey.

🚗 The A59 Clitheroe Bypass opened on New Year's Day 1971.

✿ WORSTON ✿

Worston claims a place in local 'witchlore', and it is possible that Demdike's ancestors had some connection with the village. The cottage opposite the Calf's Head Hotel has a small circular window known as 'the witches' window'. The cottage is very old, and, when a fireplace was being altered, clay effigies into which pins had been stuck were discovered, which suggests that witchcraft was once practised here. Worston Old Hall (built 1577) was dismantled c 1800, and a smaller house (illustrated above) was built on the site. The three stone heraldic shields on the porch are believed to have come from Sawley Abbey. They depict a lion rampant (the arms of Percy), the quarterly arms of England and France, and three pikes (the arms of Lacy). Behind the main street is a small meadow which was once used for bull-baiting. In the centre is a large stone with a bronze ring to which the bull would be tethered.

Crow Hill Cottage, Worston, showing the 'witches' window.'

LITTLE MEARLEY HALL is a noble 16th C. house in a lovely wooded setting. The bay window is thought to have come from the Abbot's House at Whalley Abbey.

LANE SIDE has a barn door dated 1751. ✿

All that remains of the original MEARLEY HALL are 3 huge earthworks.

MAP O.S. Explorer OL41 Forest of Bowland and Ribblesdale.

THE LOST VALLEY OF THE TREACLE MINES

5¼ MILES

ROUTE DIRECTIONS

P Sabden. Car park and toilets opposite the White Hart Inn.
Grid ref: 779 374

① Turn R past White Hart then first L. Turn R along tarmac lane (with seats at end of it). Continue along farm road. ② At cattle-grid turn R (wm). Aim for farm on hillside to locate footbridge. Climb field to gate/stile just R of farm. ③ Cross facing wall-stile, turn L and follow wall past farm. Where wall bends L a clear path slants up hillside. When it fades keep on up to stile in top LH corner. ④ Go L along lane. ⑤ At lane's lowest point take stile (FP sign) on L. Cross corner of field to a stile behind a rushy patch. Straight on to reach farm track and follow it downhill. ⑥ When track turns L leave it and go R of wall-corner to stile (wm). Turn R alongside wall. Make for gate/stile just to R of house. ⑦ Go R up drive. In 60yds go L down path between fences, then continue forward with wall on L. ⑧ Cross this wall at a step-stile and head ½ R to high wall-stile. Just beyond it cross fence-stile (wm) and bear R through two more stiles. ⑨ Go L along farm-track. Cross concrete bridge to gate L of house. Keep straight on along farm road. ⑩ Follow tarmac lane R. When it turns R go forward between farm buildings to gate/stile to L of pond, then go L through gate/stile to follow wall on L. ⑪ When wall ends keep straight on (maintain height – no path) to stile near RH corner. Make a beeline for house. ⑫ Ford stream to stile near hut (Stan's Cabin). Path goes L then swings R up to house. L of house take RISING farm road. ⑬ Just before farmyard fork R through gate and follow wall on L. Go R alongside plantation. Continue to a point where a path comes down moor from R. Here turn sharp L to follow stream down to gate. Go L along reservoir road. ⑭ When the plantation on the L ends take gate on L. From gate near small building turn R to small metal gate then follow fence on L, heading directly towards Sabden. ⑮ Before reaching farm take gate (wm) on R. Pass R of buildings, go L along reservoir road and R down lane. Keep L at fork.

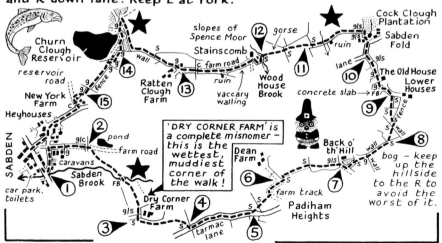

'DRY CORNER FARM' is a complete misnomer – this is the wettest, muddiest corner of the walk!

bog – keep up the hillside to the R to avoid the worst of it.

Since time immemorial the village of SABDEN has been justly famous for its thriving treacle mining industry. Though the precise location of the mines is a closely guarded secret, this walk is nonetheless of rich historical interest. Some superb Tudor farmsteads are visited on a circuit of a beautiful and secluded valley which has changed little since witches trod its byways some 400 years ago. An undulating, moderately strenuous walk. Only 1 ladder-stile, but some of the wall-stiles are a bit awkward. ½ mile on virtually traffic-free motor-roads.

TREACLE MINING

At a secret location on the slopes of Pendle Hill, and carefully concealed by tall black pudding trees, are the entrances to the deep mine which yields the raw treacle rock. This ore is locally melted down, refined and processed to produce the unique Sabden Treacle, most of which is then woven into parkin. Any treacle of inferior quality, however, is sent to a Preston flypaper manufacturer.

DEAN FARM

was built in 1574, which makes it one of the oldest houses in the area. Above the lower set of mullioned windows is a lengthy and much-eroded inscription. The house has associations with the Lancashire Witch Trials of 1612. Almost as old is **LOWER HOUSES**. Small diamonds of stained glass in its lower right-hand windows are said to have come from Whalley Abbey.

Arrangement of mullioned windows, Dean Farm.

Stainscomb

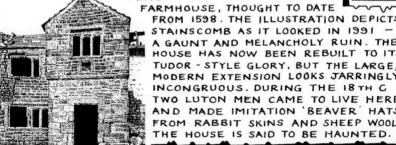

IN FRONT OF A HUGE, BRACKEN-CLAD HOLLOW IN THE FLANK OF SPENCE MOOR STANDS THIS NOBLE FARMHOUSE, THOUGHT TO DATE FROM 1598. THE ILLUSTRATION DEPICTS STAINSCOMB AS IT LOOKED IN 1991 — A GAUNT AND MELANCHOLY RUIN. THE HOUSE HAS NOW BEEN REBUILT TO ITS TUDOR-STYLE GLORY, BUT THE LARGE, MODERN EXTENSION LOOKS JARRINGLY INCONGRUOUS. DURING THE 18TH C TWO LUTON MEN CAME TO LIVE HERE AND MADE IMITATION 'BEAVER' HATS FROM RABBIT SKINS AND SHEEP WOOL. THE HOUSE IS SAID TO BE HAUNTED.

The 16-acre CHURN CLOUGH RESERVOIR is a fly fishery stocked with trout.

Between STAINSCOMB and RATTEN CLOUGH is a stretch of wall constructed of upright stone slabs. This is known as 'VACCARY WALLING' and is probably about 700 years old.

HEYHOUSES is the oldest part of Sabden village, dating back to the 16thC. The row of cottages by the brook was the scene of a chapter in Harrison Ainsworth's novel 'The Lancashire Witches'.

Pendle Witch Inn, Sabden

| MAP | O.S. Explorer OL 21 South Pennines. |

LIMESTONE LANDSCAPES

4½ MILES

P Downham. Car park and toilets at lower end of the village, near the bridge.
Grid ref: 784 441

13

ROUTE DIRECTIONS

1 From car park entrance go R (FP sign) up rough lane. Through gate/stile and forward alongside fence/wall on R. **2** When wall ends keep straight on (no path), passing RH end of line of trees. Aim for far end of Pendle Hill to locate gate in fence corner. **3** Bear R to gate/stile. Continue along foot of slope, with wall on L. Near farm path rises to run alongside fence, then wall. **4** Where wall veers L a clear, rising path continues straight ahead to stile. Descend steeply (TAKE CARE – SLIPPERY LIMESTONE) then forward to corner-stile. Straight on across next field. **5** Straight across A59 and down V-shaped path (wm) to stile. Follow fenced path round to wall-stile, go R along short lane then L along rough lane. **6** Turn L along Victoria Avenue to reach the Chatburn – Downham motor-road and turn R (Detour L to visit Chatburn). **7** Cross high bridge over A59 then take gate/stile (FP sign) on L. Follow LH field boundary round to stile into enclosed track. Cross railway bridge and continue R along sunken track. **8** Pass R of barn to gate at its far side. Turn R to follow field boundary. **9** Go R over footbridge and cross field to gateway into trees (Packhorse bridge is over to your L). Climb alongside wood. **10** Go R up road. **11** Just past a small copse on L take stile on L (FP sign). Climb diagonally R to wood then go L alongside it. **12** On passing through small gate turn R along tarmac drive to emerge into village at pub.

(Map labels:) packhorse bridge · Smithies Brook · barn · railway · concrete posts · Newfield Barn farm · copse · mind the nettles · A59 · fence · sunken path · line of Roman road · toilets · DOWNHAM · car park · CHATBURN · run for your life A59 · Piked Acre Wood · Longlands Wood · Warren Hill · Worsaw Hill 725' · line of trees · fence · wall · barn · Worsaw End (farm) · LEAD was mined on Worsaw during the 18th C.

DOWNHAM is one of Lancashire's loveliest villages.

ST. LEONARD'S CHURCH was built as recently as 1910 (except for the tower, which is 15th C.), but there has been a church on the site since at least 1283. OLD WELL HALL (illustrated) is a superb Tudor house. Downham's Assheton family features very prominently in Harrison Ainsworth's famous novel 'THE LANCASHIRE WITCHES'. In 1961 the film 'WHISTLE DOWN THE WIND' was shot on location in the village and around Worsaw End.

44

A short walk around WORSAW HILL, the most prominent of a number of smooth, rounded limestone knolls which characterise the lovely DOWNHAM countryside. Don't expect to find spectacular scars, pavements and potholes like those of the YORKSHIRE DALES; this is a gentle stroll through rich, emerald-green farmland. Ideal for a hot summer's day. No ladder-stiles. ½ mile on motor-roads.

REEF KNOLLS

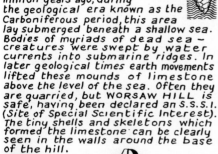

are smooth, rounded hillocks of almost pure limestone. Some 300 million years ago, during the geological era known as the Carboniferous period, this area lay submerged beneath a shallow sea. Bodies of myriads of dead sea-creatures were swept by water currents into submarine ridges. In later geological times earth movements lifted these mounds of limestone above the level of the sea. Often they are quarried, but WORSAW HILL is safe, having been declared an S.S.S.I. (Site of Special Scientific Interest). The tiny shells and skeletons which formed the limestone can be clearly seen in the walls around the base of the hill.

! THE A59 CLITHEROE BY-PASS OPENED ON NEW YEAR'S DAY 1971. IT'S A FAST AND BUSY ROAD, SO TAKE EXTREME CARE WHEN CROSSING IT AT POINT ⑤.

packhorse bridge, Smithies Brook

A perfect place for a picnic.

CHATBURN

is thought to have taken its name from St. Ceatt, or Chad. It is a thriving village with a number of excellent shops. The Parish Church, with its elegant spire, was built in 1838. Prominent in the village centre is Hudson's ice-cream shop; this building was originally a toll house on the late-18th C. Clitheroe to Skipton turnpike road. Ice-cream has been made here — to a famous but secret recipe — since 1947.

A welcoming hostelry

The RAILWAY was built by the LANCASHIRE and YORKSHIRE RAILWAY Co. It reached Chatburn by 1850 and was extended to Hellifield in the late 1870s. The line closed to regular passenger services on 10th September 1962. A typical L.Y.R. locomotive was this 2-4-2T, designed by Sir John Aspinall and built in the 1890s.

This is an area particularly rich in wildlife. There are rabbits and pheasants everywhere. Hares and foxes are common, and deer are sometimes seen — mostly sika. Birdsong fills the air, and the botanist will find much of interest. As in all limestone areas there are snails in profusion.

MAP O.S. Explorer OL 41 Forest of Bowland and Ribblesdale.

BEACON HILL

6½ MILES

14

P Sawley. Roadside space alongside river near Spread Eagle Hotel.
Grid ref: 777 466
There is also some parking space at the road junction near Sawley Bridge - point ②.

ROUTE DIRECTIONS

① From Spread Eagle take Bolton-by-Bowland road. ② L at fork then R to Friends' Meeting House. Pass to immediate L of garage (looks private), climb through plantation and make for stile well to R of house. Forward with hedge on L. ③ Straight on past LH of two ash trees. Drop to stile and footbridge. Climb field to stile near top RH corner. ④ Climb LH edge of fields. ⑤ Bear R to pass immediately in front of house to flagged path across lawn. Cross yard and cattle-grid and up farm road. ⑥ At last farm building take stile (wm) up on R. Forward with fence to stile, then cross field to go through old gateposts at RH corner. From next stile bear slightly L uphill. Pass L of farm and follow wall on L round to enclosed track. ⑦ Go L along road. Take gate (FP sign) on R. Climb along LH side of shallow gully then follow wall on R to descend enclosed track. ⑧ Turn L (wm) along clear path near LH edge of plantation. ⑨ Turn R along lane then L through gate (BW sign). Clear path leads to gate by narrow strip of woodland, continues by wall and eventually becomes a farm road. ⑩ Turn L at junction. Follow lane into Grindleton. ⑪ Just past bus terminus turn L (FP sign) up track, then R to follow Back Lane down to main road. Go L along it. ⑫ Turn R at school. At end of lane go forward along enclosed track. In open field turn L (RW sign) and cont. below

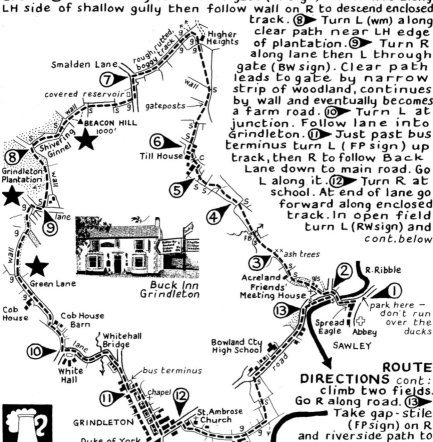

ROUTE DIRECTIONS cont: climb two fields. Go R along road. ⑬ Take gap-stile (FP sign) on R and riverside path to Sawley Bridge.

Higher Heights

Smalden Lane

covered reservoir

gateposts

⑦ rough, rutted, boggy track

wall

BEACON HILL 1000'

Shivering Ginnel

⑧ Grindleton Plantation

⑥ Till House

⑤

④

FB

⑨ lane

ash trees

Green Lane

③ Acreland Friends' Meeting House

② R. Ribble

① park here — don't run over the ducks

Cob House

Cob House Barn

Whitehall Bridge

⑩ White Hall

lane

bus terminus

⑪ chapel ⑫

St. Ambrose Church

GRINDLETON

Duke of York

Buck Inn

Bowland Cty High School

⑬ Spread Eagle Abbey SAWLEY

Fields House R. Ribble

Buck Inn Grindleton

46

A rapturous ramble from the lush pastures of the RIBBLE VALLEY into the south-eastern fringes of the magnificent hill country known as the FOREST OF BOWLAND. The outward half - from SAWLEY to the top of BEACON HILL - involves over 800' of uphill work, but it's very gradual, with no steep gradients. Varied terrain, including pathless pastures, green lanes and forest tracks. Only 1 ladder-stile (and that's a diddy one). 1¼ miles on quiet motor-roads.

Those who tread softly in the vicinity of the plantations may be lucky enough to catch a glimpse of the **SIKA DEER**, though it is a shy creature and rarely ventures far from the cover of the forest. The sika is not a native British deer; it was introduced into parks from Japan during the 17thC., and is now established in the wild in this and a few other areas. In its spotted summer coat it resembles the slightly larger fallow deer. In winter the sika is plain and grey.

Spread Eagle Hotel

★ SAWLEY ★

An attractive village with several interesting buildings. Sawley is best known for its abbey ruins.

SOME FACTS ABOUT SAWLEY ABBEY

• Founded by Cistercians in 1147. • Ruins reveal a lack of wealth - built with a mixture of black shale and boulder stones. • Struggled to compete with a rival abbey founded at Whalley in 1296. • Housed only 21 monks when dissolved by Henry VIII 1536. • William Trafford, the last abbot, was executed 10 March 1537 for his involvement in the Pilgrimage of Grace (a rebellion to re-establish the monastic way of life). • The arch over a nearby field gateway has no connection with the abbey; it was built in the 1840s.

BEACON HILL is of modest height, but the view from its O.S. column (S 5159) is quite remarkable. To the SE dear old Pendle smiles or frowns (depending on the weather) at us across the lush Ribble Valley. The northern aspect presents a sweeping panorama from the dark fells of Bowland around to the shapely peaks of the Yorkshire Dales, with Ingleborough and Penyghent highly prominent.

lych-gate, Parish Church

GRINDLETON

takes its name from the bygone local industry of quarrying and the making of grindstones. It is a place of numerous alleyways and ginnels. Many of the houses were originally weavers' cottages, dating from the days when all cloth was produced on handlooms and transported by packhorse over the hills to market.

Featured on the sign is the hen harrier, a rare bird of prey which breeds in a few of Bowland's wildest localities.

Forest of Bowland

| MAP | O.S. Explorer OL 41 Forest of Bowland and Ribblesdale. |

PENDLE HILL
FROM BARLEY

5 MILES

P Barley. Car park, toilets and small info. centre/shop at S end of village.

Grid ref : 823 403

ROUTE DIRECTIONS

① From car park entrance go R to junction and go up lane to R of village hall. Follow it past lower reservoir and on up the valley, ignoring two farm roads rising R, to a gate/stile below upper reservoir dam. Climb to R of dam and continue alongside reservoir between wall and fence. **②** Through swing-gate and continue alongside wall, which is now on your L. From gate in crosswall path rises steeply to R then levels out to reach Boar Clough (identified by its lone hawthorn). **③** Cross small stream. Ignore path rising R. Pass L of wooden barrier and in about 100yds, at PW sign, turn sharp R up thin path which soon becomes broader as it climbs LH side of clough. **④** Cross the stream and continue alongside it (wm). In about 200yds, at a cairn, path bears R, away from stream. Follow cairned path. It eventually swings L to join another path coming up from R. **⑤** At summit keep straight ahead (N) towards wall and ladder-stile. DON'T cross the stile, but turn R to descend by wall to guidestone and stile. DON'T cross this either, but turn R to descend 'constructed' path. **⑥** From gate below wall-corner fork R (FP Barley 1·8km) to gate at far side of buildings. Descend LH side of field to gate (wm). **⑦** In next field bear slightly R. Clear path develops in depression. Go through gate in wall and L down wall-side to another gate. **⑧** Go R along cart-track then L through swing-gate. Follow fence on L, ignoring a cattle-grid, to path on RH side of wall. **⑨** Turn L along lane. Where lane bends L go R over footbridge, then turn L and, keeping parallel with stream, descend into village. Turn R along road. At Pendle Inn go through gap in wall on L to follow path to car park.

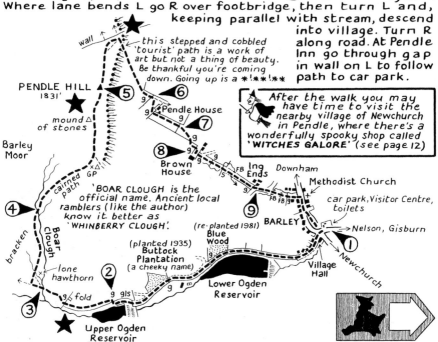

this stepped and cobbled 'tourist' path is a work of art but not a thing of beauty. Be thankful you're coming down. Going up is a *!**!**

After the walk you may have time to visit the nearby village of Newchurch in Pendle, where there's a wonderfully spooky shop called **'WITCHES GALORE'** (see page 12)

PENDLE HILL
1831'

mound △ of stones

Barley Moor

cairned path
GP

'BOAR CLOUGH is the official name. Ancient local ramblers (like the author) know it better as 'WHINBERRY CLOUGH'.

bracken

Boar Clough

lone hawthorn

fold

Upper Ogden Reservoir

Pendle House

Brown House

Ing Ends

FB

Downham

Methodist Church

car park, Visitor Centre, toilets

BARLEY

(re-planted 1981) Blue Wood

(planted 1935) Buttock Plantation (a cheeky name)

Lower Ogden Reservoir

Village Hall

Newchurch

→ Nelson, Gisburn

48

A great walk with a real 'witch country flavour,' where one will experience the full impact of PENDLE'S wild, brooding grandeur. Moderately strenuous (1075' of ascent), the hardest bit being the initial stage of the climb up BOAR CLOUGH. The route, which for all but the first half-mile coincides with the PENDLE WAY, is well-waymarked and easy to follow in normal conditions, BUT PENDLE'S VAST UPPER SLOPES CAN BE VERY CONFUSING IN MIST. No ladder-stiles. Motor-road walking negligible. Magnificent views.

BARLEY

The Barley Mow Restaurant

The size of the car park is an indication of the popularity of this small, attractive village with hikers and tourists. Barley began life as a 13th C. vaccary, and was called 'Barelegh' (infertile lea or meadow). It has always been a farming community, but in Victorian times there were two cotton mills here — at Barley Green and Narrowgates. The former, which is passed on this walk, was wrecked by floods in the 1880s, and is now a Water Authority filter station. The Pendle Inn (built 1930) dispenses a gradely pint.

BEWARE LOW FLYING WITCHES

OGDEN RESERVOIRS

The two reservoirs provide drinking water for the Nelson area. LOWER OGDEN RESERVOIR was completed in 1914. It has a surface area of 21·12 acres, a maximum depth of 59', and holds 157·5 million gallons. UPPER OGDEN RESERVOIR is older, being completed in 1906. It has an area of 7·01 acres, a maximum depth of 58', and a capacity of 54·5 million gallons. The illustration depicts the Lower Reservoir

PLEASE KEEP BONZO ON A LEAD DURING THE NESTING SEASON (APRIL – JUNE)

PENDLE

The top of the hill is a vast plateau of peat hags and coarse grasses. At any time of day, whate'er the weather or season, SOMEBODY will be on Pendle and, as most of these somebodies will be ascending from Barley via the 'tourist path', you are most unlikely to be alone from the summit onwards. Pendle stands in splendid isolation, and thus commands spectacular views – a magnificent panorama of infinite variety and charm.

A Pendle Way cairn

DOWNHAM

Guidepost at top of 'tourist' path

MAP O.S. Explorer OL 21 South Pennines **OR** O.S. Explorer OL 41 Forest of Bowland and Ribblesdale.

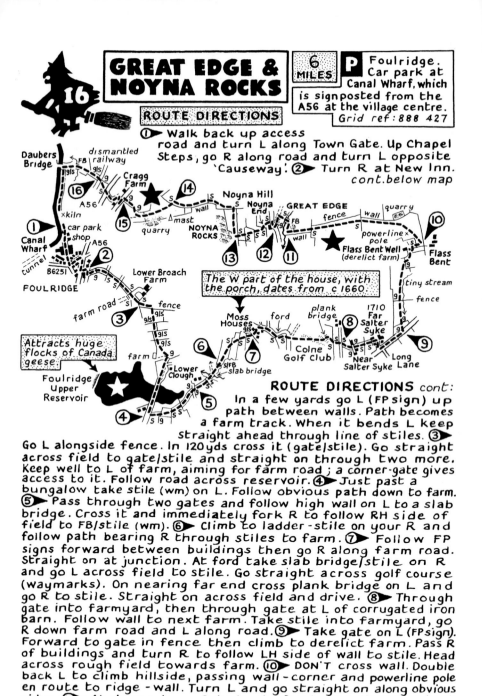

GREAT EDGE & NOYNA ROCKS

16

6 MILES

P Foulridge. Car park at Canal Wharf, which is signposted from the A56 at the village centre.
Grid ref: 888 427

ROUTE DIRECTIONS

① Walk back up access road and turn L along Town Gate. Up Chapel Steps, go R along road and turn L opposite 'Causeway'. ② Turn R at New Inn. *cont. below map*

Daubers Bridge
dismantled railway
FB
9/s 9/s
Cragg Farm
9
A56
xkiln
car park shop
A56
Canal Wharf
tunnel
B6251
FOULRIDGE
② ③
Lower Broach Farm
fence
9/s
9/s
9/s
9/s
farm road
9/s
farm

Attracts huge flocks of Canada geese

Foulridge Upper Reservoir
④ ⑤ ⑥ ⑦
Lower Clough
slab bridge

Noyna Hill
Noyna End
wall
mast
quarry
NOYNA ROCKS
⑬ ⑫ ⑪
Moss Houses
ford
plank bridge
Colne Golf Club
Near Salter Syke
Long Salter Syke Lane

GREAT EDGE
FB
fence
wall
wall
powerline pole
Flass Bent Well (derelict farm)
⑩
Flass Bent
tiny stream
fence
1710 Far Salter Syke
⑧ ⑨

quarry

The W part of the house, with the porch, dates from c 1660

ROUTE DIRECTIONS cont:

In a few yards go L (FP sign) up path between walls. Path becomes a farm track. When it bends L keep straight ahead through line of stiles. ③ Go L alongside fence. In 120yds cross it (gate/stile). Go straight across field to gate/stile and straight on through two more. Keep well to L of farm, aiming for farm road; a corner-gate gives access to it. Follow road across reservoir. ④ Just past a bungalow take stile (wm) on L. Follow obvious path down to farm. ⑤ Pass through two gates and follow high wall on L to a slab bridge. Cross it and immediately fork R to follow RH side of field to FB/stile (wm). ⑥ Climb to ladder-stile on your R and follow path bearing R through stiles to farm. ⑦ Follow FP signs forward between buildings then go R along farm road. Straight on at junction. At ford take slab bridge/stile on R and go L across field to stile. Go straight across golf course (waymarks). On nearing far end cross plank bridge on L and go R to stile. Straight on across field and drive. ⑧ Through gate into farmyard, then through gate at L of corrugated iron barn. Follow wall to next farm. Take stile into farmyard, go R down farm road and L along road. ⑨ Take gate on L (FPsign). Forward to gate in fence then climb to derelict farm. Pass R of buildings and turn R to follow LH side of wall to stile. Head across rough field towards farm. ⑩ DON'T cross wall. Double back L to climb hillside, passing wall-corner and powerline pole en route to ridge-wall. Turn L and go straight on along obvious ridge. ⑪ At stream turn R to locate footbridge. Climb steep bank (wm) and straight on up to green track. Go L along it (wm). ⑫ Turn R up lane. In 25 paces take stile (FP sign) on L. Go uphill with wall on L. Take stile (wm) on L, then head *cont. on next page*

50

CANAL WHARF at FOULRIDGE, an absorbing place for students of industrial archaeology, makes an interesting starting - point for this pleasant excursion into the upland country of the LANCS/YORKS border. Undulating and moderately strenuous, with some rough ground in the vicinity of FLASS BENT. Expect oodles of mud in wet weather 3 ladder - stiles. ⅓ mile on motor - roads. Superb views. CAREFUL REFERENCE TO MAP AND/OR ROUTE DIRECTIONS IS REQUIRED IN ORDER TO AVOID GOING ASTRAY ON THIS RATHER COMPLEX ROUTE WITH ITS MANY TWISTS AND TURNS.

ROUTE DIRECTIONS cont : R through line of stiles to reach foot of sloping outcrops. ⑬▶ Turn R to climb RH side of field to stile. Turn L and follow wall on L. ⑭▶ Go L through step-stile and forward, keeping R of quarry to follow green path through gateway in wall. In 50yds fork R on lesser path to gate by hollies. Follow wall (BW sign) down to road. ⑮▶ Go L for 20yds then sharp R into Cragg Farm. Turn L down track (setts initially). Cross main road and bear R to sunken track at field - corner. Cross old railway. ⑯▶ Drop to footbridge, bear L to canal bridge and L along towpath.

CANAL WHARF was built in 1815 to handle cotton, coal, limestone and other goods coming to and from Colne by barge. Now it is used solely for recreation, and the Marton Emperor takes sightseers on canal cruises and through the famous Foulridge Tunnel, which is dead straight, almost a mile long, and took 5 years to build (opened 1796). It has no internal towpath, and 'leggers' had to lie on planks fixed to the barges and 'walk' along the tunnel wall, pushing the barge as they went. This dangerous practice ceased in the 1880s with the introduction of the steam tug. On 24 Sept 1912 Buttercup the cow fell into the canal and swam through the tunnel to Foulridge, where she was rescued and revived with whisky at the Hole in the Wall pub. Near the car park is a reconstructed limekiln. Refreshments are available at the shop, which occupies the former stables.

The lonely and forlorn ruins of Flass Bent Well

The two large RESERVOIRS at Foulridge were built in the early 19th C. to supply water into the canal. The lower reservoir is known as LAKE BURWAIN

THE **NEW INN** (point ②) IS REPUTED TO BE PENDLE'S MOST HAUNTED PUB. ● **NOYNA ROCKS** has long been a favourite picnic site for local families. Kids love to scramble over the sloping gritstone slabs.

Noyna End Farm

Stile at point ⑭ (easily missed)

| MAP | O.S. Explorer OL 21 South Pennines. |

WADDINGTON

6 MILES

P Brungerley Bridge, on the B6478 Clitheroe to Waddington road. Small layby 100 yds north of bridge.

Grid ref: 738 429

17

ROUTE DIRECTIONS

① Walk down road to cross bridge and in 90 yds turn L into park. Follow main lower path. Ignore all paths rising R. ② Fork L (RW sign) off main path down to stile. Follow riverside path to Bradford Bridge. Cross bridge and follow road up into village. ③ At T-junction turn R then L (BW sign) through farmyard. As soon as you've passed all buildings go ½ R off farm track. Climb, passing through line of small hawthorns, to gate on skyline. ④ Straight on up next field to gate at its far RH corner (adjacent to wood). Go L along tarmac lane. ⑤ At farmhouse go L through a gate and forward through another. Cross field diagonally R (aim for distant mast). From corner-stile follow powerline to another. Follow stony path down into wood. ⑥ Ford stream and go sharp L up to Drake House. Pass R of buildings. Take 2nd gate (wm) on R and climb to gate/stile at top LH corner. ⑦ Cross to stile (wm). Bypass buildings ahead by using field to their R. ⑧ Turn L down lane. At house take gate (FP sign) on R. Cross field diagonally L to corner-stile and ditto in next field. ⑨ Go R along track by high wall. Pass R of houses then bear slightly R (wm) on grassy path (ignore gate (wm) on R). Cross tiny stream and take stile up on L. Follow hedge on R then straight on along farm road. ⑩ When farm road bends R go straight on down thin path into trees then L over high wall-stile. Follow edge of wood until a fence deflects you L to gate/stile. Keep straight on down to pass L of hospital. ⑪ Turn R into village, L down main street and R along Waddow View. At T-junction turn L to follow road for about ½ mile. ⑫ Take gate on L and follow grassy cart-track. At FP sign go L up to gate/stile then forward alongside wall. ⑬ Go L along main drive. On nearing road fork R to gate/stile. Car is just down to your R.

(Map labels:)

⑥ ford gls
⑧ Hancocks
Brocklehurst
⑦ Drake House ⑤
Drakehouse Wood
⑩ Dove Sike ⑨
Feazer Farm ④ gls
Hospital Wood gls
small hawthorns farm track
gls
Pillings
hospital
Three Millstones Inn ③
⑪ WEST BRADFORD
Parish Church WADDINGTON Hall
memorial gardens
Bradford Bridge
River Ribble
Oaken Fields
wooded limestone knolls ⑬
camp site
⑫ ① Waddow Hall
B6478
Brungerley Bridge
Park here
Cross Hill Quarry (nature reserve)
RW
② public park
toilets

WADDOW HALL HAS BEEN OWNED BY THE GIRL GUIDES ASSOCIATION SINCE 1928.

52

A visit to WADDINGTON is an absolute *must*. Steeped in history and tended with pride by its residents, this gem of a village is undoubtedly one of the prettiest in LANCASHIRE. An easy and peaceful walk through lush, green, gently undulating pastures at the very heart of the RIBBLE VALLEY. No ladder-stiles, but a high wall-stile at point ⑩ may be awkward for dog-walkers. 1½ miles on motor-roads. Refreshments are available at both WEST BRADFORD and WADDINGTON.

BRUNGERLEY

During the troubled times of the Wars of the Roses the Lancastrian King Henry VI found refuge at Waddington Hall. However, his presence there was discovered by the Yorkists, and in attempting to flee he was captured at Brungerley stepping-stones (there was no bridge then). It is said that he was made to ride to London sitting back-to-front on his horse. A flimsy bridge built in 1801 was soon destroyed by floods, and was replaced by the present bridge in 1816. CROSS HILL QUARRY, a 19th C. limestone quarry abandoned c.1900, is now a nature reserve with many lime-loving plants and a profusion of butterflies.

HENRY VI
1421-71

Along this stretch of river you may see the OYSTERCATCHER, a black and white wader with distinctive orange legs and bill. It doesn't catch oysters, either in the Ribble or anywhere else.

WEST BRADFORD

IS A PLEASANT LITTLE VILLAGE WHICH HAS ENJOYED A LONG AND LARGELY UNEVENTFUL HISTORY. THE NAME 'BRADFORD' – A WIDE, SHALLOW CROSSING PLACE (OF THE RIBBLE). THE COTTAGE ILLUSTRATED IS A TYPICAL EXAMPLE OF WEST BRADFORD'S MANY ATTRACTIVE AND WELL-KEPT HOUSES. IN RECENT YEARS WEST BRADFORD HAS GROWN CONSIDERABLY, AND THE MODERN 'COMMUTER' HOUSING HAS TO SOME EXTENT ALTERED THE CHARACTER OF THE VILLAGE. IN SEPTEMBER 1931 MAHATMA GANDHI, THE ILLUSTRIOUS INDIAN STATESMAN, STAYED AT HEYS FARM WHILST ON A FACT-FINDING TOUR OF LANCASHIRE'S COTTON MILLS.

GANDHI (1869-1948)

WADDINGTON

A stream bisects this lovely village, which is dominated by the 16th C tower of ST. HELEN'S CHURCH. St.Helen (c 248-328) was the mother of Constantine the Great. The church (apart from the tower) was rebuilt 1824-8 and again 1898-1901. The ALMSHOUSES, known as the 'Widows' Hospital,' were built in 1700 (the gateway is original). Later they were rebuilt and grouped around a green with a small chapel. The villages most eye-catching feature lies alongside the main street – the beautiful GARDEN OF REMEMBRANCE, with its chuckling stream, tiny bridge, sundial and floral displays.

A resident of Drake House

MAP   O.S. Explorer OL 41 Forest of Bowland and Ribblesdale.

THE LEAFY LANES OF RIMINGTON

18

P Rimington Small car park opposite Springfield Farm near Black Bull Hotel. Grid ref: 805 458

BEWARE FRISKY COWS

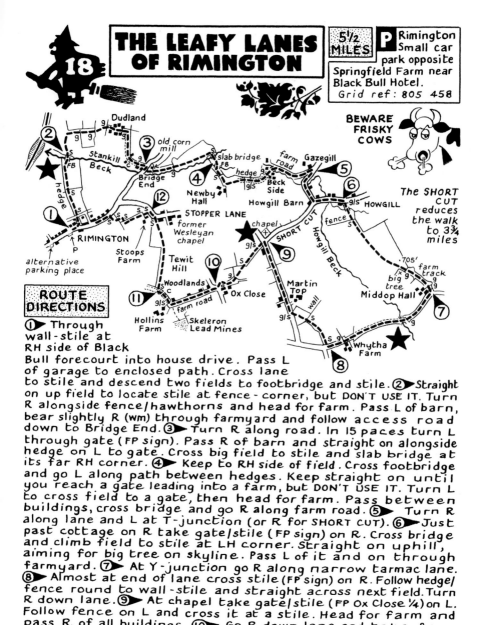

The SHORT CUT reduces the walk to 3¾ miles

ROUTE DIRECTIONS

① Through wall-stile at RH side of Black Bull forecourt into house drive. Pass L of garage to enclosed path. Cross lane to stile and descend two fields to footbridge and stile. **②** Straight on up field to locate stile at fence-corner, but DON'T USE IT. Turn R alongside fence/hawthorns and head for farm. Pass L of barn, bear slightly R (wm) through farmyard and follow access road down to Bridge End. **③** Turn R along road. In 15 paces turn L through gate (FP sign). Pass R of barn and straight on alongside hedge on L to gate. Cross big field to stile and slab bridge at its far RH corner. **④** Keep to RH side of field. Cross footbridge and go L along path between hedges. Keep straight on until you reach a gate leading into a farm, but DON'T USE IT. Turn L to cross field to a gate, then head for farm. Pass between buildings, cross bridge and go R along farm road. **⑤** Turn R along lane and L at T-junction (or R for SHORT CUT). **⑥** Just past cottage on R take gate/stile (FP sign) on R. Cross bridge and climb field to stile at LH corner. Straight on uphill, aiming for big tree on skyline. Pass L of it and on through farmyard. **⑦** At Y-junction go R along narrow tarmac lane. **⑧** Almost at end of lane cross stile (FP sign) on R. Follow hedge/fence round to wall-stile and straight across next field. Turn R down lane. **⑨** At chapel take gate/stile (FP Ox Close ¼) on L. Follow fence on L and cross it at a stile. Head for farm and pass R of all buildings. **⑩** Go R down lane and take farm road to L of house called 'Woodlands'. Just before reaching farmyard take gate/stile on R to cart-track. **⑪** 50yds past cattle-grid take stile near gate on R. Straight on, with fence on L, then descend to stile on L of large garage. Go L along road. **⑫** Take stile on L (FP Rimington ¼). Straight on over stile. At end of next field cross stile on R, turn L to a corner-stile, then ½R to hedge-stile. Go L through village.

Nestling among the folds of the undulating limestone country to the north of PENDLE lie a host of tranquil villages and tiny hamlets linked by a complex network of narrow, leafy lanes. This is excellent rambling country, best sampled during late spring and summer when birdsong fills the air and the hedgerows are bedecked with flowers. No ladder-stiles. Motor-road walking negligible. Not a good walk for dogs — too much farm livestock.

RIMINGTON

A small, linear village, peaceful and pretty, and of sufficient antiquity to have been mentioned in the 1086 Domesday Survey. Nearly all the houses are strung along the north side of the road, facing Pendle Hill. There is a pub but no church, and the only shop is, somewhat incongruously, a high-class fashion house. The pub, which contains a fascinating collection of railway memorabilia, became the 'Black Bull' in the 1940s; prior to that it was 'The Haven.' Many of the old farm barns at Rimington have in recent years been tastefully converted into very desirable private residences.

Convolvulus, or bindweed, grows in profusion in the hedgerows.

★

The author, having spent his childhood here (at the house called 'Fern Lea'), has a special affection for this walk, for all these fields and woods, lanes and streams were his idyllic playground.

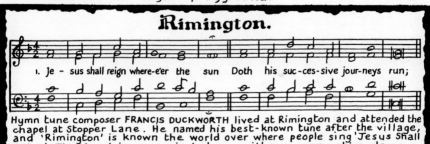

Rimington.

1. Je-sus shall reign where-e'er the sun Doth his suc-ces-sive jour-neys run;

Hymn tune composer FRANCIS DUCKWORTH lived at Rimington and attended the chapel at Stopper Lane. He named his best-known tune after the village, and 'Rimington' is known the world over where people sing 'Jesus Shall Reign.' The chapel is now a private house with a commemorative plaque.

flies swift away

Some joker has seen fit to tamper with this sign at Gazegill

Max speed 120

Stoops Farm   Stopper Lane

Sundial, Martin Top chapel.

MIDDOP HALL is a fine 16th C. farmhouse. High in the front wall of the barn can be seen a fragment of masonry from Sawley Abbey.

MAP	O.S. Explorer OL 21 South Pennines **OR** O.S. Explorer OL 41 Forest of Bowland and Ribblesdale.

A CANALSIDE WALK IN CRAVEN

19

5 MILES

P Car park, picnic area by the locks at Greenberfield Bridge, Greenberfield Lane, off the B6252 Barnoldswick – Thornton – in – Craven road. *Grid ref: 888 482*

ROUTE DIRECTIONS

① Go up to canal and go L along towpath, which at Bridge Nº 158 crosses to other bank. ② Just around LH bend of canal take step-stile (PW sign). Go up to high wire fence and follow it R to gate/stile. Turn L to another gate/stile. ③ Go L along road. Almost opposite main gates of factory take (FP sign) on R. Climb to stile into churchyard. Leave churchyard by main gate, immediately turn L then L again to follow enclosed path down to stone footbridge. ④ Straight on across golf course, passing L of small plantation and through a narrow plantation beyond (PW sign). Straight on past powerline pole to cross farm track and stile, then head for church. Cross stile in far RH corner and go R by hedge to join road. ⑤ Go through stile (wm) opposite church and head just to L of farm. Cross farm track via gates, bear L through gated stile (PW sign) then keep straight on. ⑥ At a hollow (near an old windpump) swing R and head for gate/stile at far corner. Straight on through gate/stile in wall and maintain level course across big field to stile (wm) near its LH corner. ⑦ Head for large tree on skyline. Just to R of it are two stiles – take the RH one. Keep to RH side of field to gate/stile then bear L past powerline pole. Keep L of house and forward along its access drive. ⑧ At T-junction take facing stile (FP sign). Keep straight on, then bear L down to gate/stile at corner. Follow wall to canal. ⑨ Cross bridge if you wish to visit Canal Shop. Otherwise turn R to follow towpath (crossing canal at Bridge Nº 153) for a 1½ mile stroll back to Greenberfield.

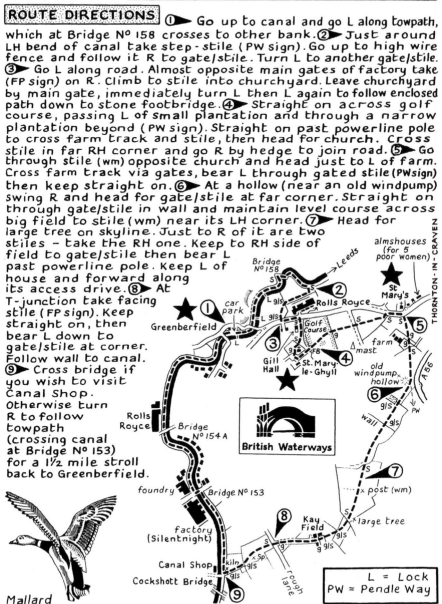

Mallard

L = Lock
PW = Pendle Way

A most unusual and interesting walk of extreme contrasts. From GREENBERFIELD, the summit of the LEEDS/LIVERPOOL CANAL, there are lovely views across the hummocky limestone landscapes of WEST CRAVEN. Two beautiful old churches will be admired before we conclude the walk by following the towpath as it winds fascinatingly through industrial BARLICK (Barnoldswick). No ladder-stiles. Motor-road walking negligible. The walk briefly trespasses into YORKSHIRE between the footbridge at point ④ and the old windpump near point ⑥.

THE LEEDS - LIVERPOOL ★ CANAL ★

is, at 127 miles, the longest in Britain. It has 91 locks, and, when finally opened, in 1816, it had taken 40 years to complete and had cost £1¼ million. The canal brought prosperity to places like Barlick. Raw cotton for the textile industry came up from Liverpool, and the canal also transported limestone, coal and other vital supplies. The locks at GREENBERFIELD raise the canal to its summit level of 487'. By the early 1960s freight had virtually disappeared from the canal, and it is now widely used for tourism and recreation.

The famous **ROLLS ROYCE** firm took over the early jet engine work from Rover in 1943, and it was at Barlick that the world-beating RB 211 engine was developed ('RB' stands for 'Rolls - Barnoldswick').

GILL HALL, a 16th C. house, was once used as a rectory.

THE LOVELY CHURCH OF **ST. MARY-LE-GHYLL** (OR LE-GILL) IS SO NAMED BECAUSE IT STANDS ON THE EDGE OF A RAVINE. CISTERCIAN MONKS FROM FOUNTAINS CAME HERE IN 1147 TO BUILD A MONASTERY, BUT VARIOUS ADVERSITIES FORCED THEM, WITHIN 5 YEARS, TO MOVE TO A NEW SITE AT KIRKSTALL (LEEDS). MONKS RETURNED FROM KIRKSTALL c1160 TO BUILD THE FIRST GILL CHURCH. THE HUGE TOWER WAS ADDED IN THE 16TH C. (IT IS DATED MCCCCCXXIIII). THE INTERIOR HAS MANY ANCIENT FEATURES, INCLUDING SUPERB JACOBEAN BOX-PEWS AND A THREE-DECKER PULPIT WITH AN OVER-HEAD SOUNDING BOARD. THE OLDEST TOMBSTONE IN THE CHURCHYARD IS DATED 1609.

ST. MARY'S CHURCH, Thornton, largely dates from the 15th C. The tower is early 16th C. In the churchyard is a curious octagonal well-house bearing the date MDCCLXIV (1764). A little further along the road stand the almshouses of 1815.

St. Mary's Thornton

★

To the best of the author's knowledge, Barnoldswick is the only place-name in the country with twelve letters all different.

MAP   O.S. Explorer OL 21 South Pennines

(This is probably the most useless piece of information in the book).

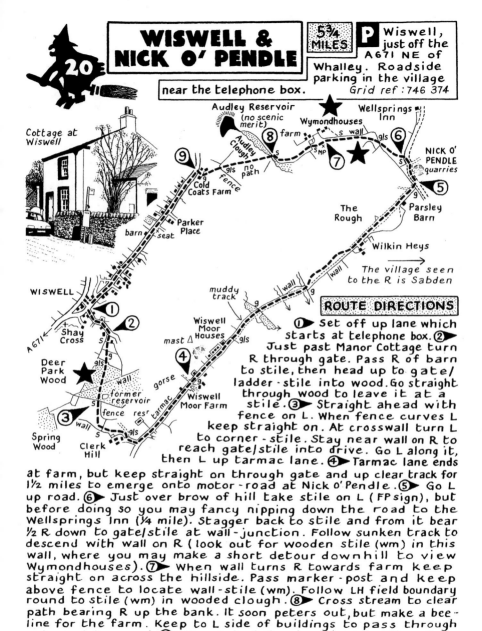

WISWELL & NICK O' PENDLE

5¾ MILES

P Wiswell, just off the A671 NE of Whalley. Roadside parking in the village near the telephone box.   Grid ref : 746 374

20

Audley Reservoir *(no scenic merit)*

Wellsprings Inn

Wymondhouses

⑧ farm   s wall   gls ⑥

Audley Clough   s   MP   ⑦   ★

NICK O' PENDLE quarries

⑨   gls   no path   fence

Cold Coats Farm   g

Cottage at Wiswell

⑤

The Rough

Parsley Barn

barn   seat   Parker Place

Wilkin Heys

The village seen to the R is Sabden

WISWELL

muddy track   wall   wall

① ②

Shay Cross   s   g   gls

A671

Wiswell Moor Houses   gls

mast △   ④

Deer Park Wood   gls   g   gorse   tarmac

wall   former reservoir   s   fence   res'r   Wiswell Moor Farm

③   wall   s   gls   tarmac

Spring Wood   Clerk Hill

ROUTE DIRECTIONS

① Set off up lane which starts at telephone box. ② Just past Manor Cottage turn R through gate. Pass R of barn to stile, then head up to gate/ladder-stile into wood. Go straight through wood to leave it at a stile. ③ Straight ahead with fence on L. When fence curves L keep straight on. At crosswall turn L to corner-stile. Stay near wall on R to reach gate/stile into drive. Go L along it, then L up tarmac lane. ④ Tarmac lane ends at farm, but keep straight on through gate and up clear track for 1½ miles to emerge onto motor-road at Nick o' Pendle. ⑤ Go L up road. ⑥ Just over brow of hill take stile on L (FP sign), but before doing so you may fancy nipping down the road to the Wellsprings Inn (¼ mile). Stagger back to stile and from it bear ½ R down to gate/stile at wall-junction. Follow sunken track to descend with wall on R (look out for wooden stile (wm) in this wall, where you may make a short detour downhill to view Wymondhouses). ⑦ When wall turns R towards farm keep straight on across the hillside. Pass marker-post and keep above fence to locate wall-stile (wm). Follow LH field boundary round to stile (wm) in wooded clough. ⑧ Cross stream to clear path bearing R up the bank. It soon peters out, but make a bee-line for the farm. Keep to L side of buildings to pass through gate and farmyard. ⑨ Turn L to follow lane back to Wiswell.

WISWELL HALL FARM, near **SHAY CROSS**, stands close to the site of the demolished **WISWELL HALL**. The Hall was the birthplace of **JOHN PASLEW**, the last abbot of Whalley, who in 1537 was executed for his part in the Pilgrimage of Grace.

58

This bracing walk, with extensive and ever-changing views, takes us from wooded limestone hills to the bleak gritstone of PENDLE'S western slopes. Much of the walk is on potentially muddy farm tracks, so ideally it should be done during a dry summer spell. Hot and weary wayfarers will relish the sublime prospect of a pint at the midway – and highest – point. Only 1 ladder-stile, but some of the wall-stiles are a bit awkward. ¾ mile on quiet motor-roads.

Cottages at Wiswell

WISWELL

or 'Wizzle' as it is known locally, is a tranquil, sleepy sort of place, with some affluent-looking houses and some attractively renovated old cottages. It was not always so quiet; in 1870 Wiswell was populated by 465 good souls, many of whom found employment either at the quarries on Wiswell Moor or the mill at nearby Barrow. The village, which was first recorded in a charter of 1193 in the reign of Richard I, is said to have grown around an old spring known in the 12th C as 'Wisa's Well'. Liquid refreshment nowadays may be found at the Freemasons Arms, which is hidden away down Vicarage Fold (opposite the 'phone box)

CLERK HILL, A CHARMING GEORGIAN MANSION, WAS BUILT BETWEEN 1715 AND 1772. ILLUSTRATED LEFT IS THE COACH HOUSE, WHICH BEARS THE LATTER DATE.

PARSLEY BARN may take its name from John Paslew, the last abbot of Whalley Abbey (see previous page)

• • •

WYMONDHOUSES

THE FIRST CONGREGATIONAL CHURCH IN NORTH EAST LANCASHIRE WAS FOUNDED HERE BY THOMAS JOLLIE IN 1667

When, in the days of religious persecution, the fiery and controversial Rev. Thomas Jollie, Minister of Altham, was expelled from his church, he held secret services for those non-conformists who cared to join him at remote Wymondhouses. The 17th C farmhouse carries a commemorative plaque above its door.

• • •

Cold Coats Farm has a window from Whalley Abbey in its gable end, and decorated masonry from the Abbey in its walls.

THE SHAY CROSS aka the 'Weeping Cross' is a restored shaft set in an ancient socket. It marks what was a halting place for funeral processions on the way to Whalley churchyard.

MAP | O.S. Explorer 19 West Pennine Moors.

ROUGHLEE & THE WATER MEETINGS

5¾ MILES

P Higherford. Go along Foreside, a narrow lane which starts between Higherford Bridge and Mill and runs alongside Pendle Water. There is space to park a few cars at the end of the lane.

Grid ref : 862 403

ROUTE DIRECTIONS

① Walk back towards main road. Turn R into ginnel (by entrance to Brook Dell House). Climb wooden steps to corner-stile. **②** Cross field diagonally to redundant stile at top end of line of hawthorns. Turn L and cross field to stile in hedge. Straight on through line of stiles, crossing two farm roads and a tiny stream, then follow fence up to stile. **③** Go R up lane. In 150 yds take stile (wm) on L. Cross footbridge and bear slightly L to follow LH side of hedge. Keep straight on up to farm. **④** Over fence-stile, bear L to small gate, then climb with holly hedge on L. From wall-stile keep straight on down to guidepost and bear L to stepping-stones. Go L along road into village. **⑤** Returning from Bay Horse take first lane on L and immediately turn R. Pass Hall and go L up farm road, through yard and on to gate/ stile at white house. **⑥** Sunken path overgrown and boggy. Walk on LH side of it. At last holly turn L across field to gate. Follow wall on R (crossing it midway by stile) up to stile into wood. Go ½ R, climbing gently, to stile just above level of house. **⑦** Follow wall past house and L downhill. A fence-stile admits to plantation, but path is badly overgrown, so descend farm track. **⑧** Take stile on R at bottom of plantation, cross footbridge and up through gap in hollies. Just before reaching house turn L to gate. Use stile to R of farmhouse and out along tarmac drive. **⑨** Turn R along lane and L (FP sign) up farm road (FOR SHORT CUT TO POINT ⑭ STAY ON LANE). **⑩** Pass L of farm (yellow arrows) and continue uphill alongside wall on R. **⑪** Turn R along farm road. Look for stile 5 yards from wall-corner on R. Descend towards farm. **⑫** From wall-stile keep to LH side of field to stile just above conifers. Go through farmyard and down access road. **⑬** Where it turns L take fence stile on R and drop to stile just below gate in fence on L. Aim for big house to locate stile at bottom of field, then descend slightly R to stream. Don't cross it; turn R and follow it to road bridge. **⑭** Cross bridge

cont. on next page

Burn Moor
barn
Jackson's House (farm)
g/s
⑪
⑫
Burn Moor c End
fence
barn
Higher Wheathead
farm road
⑩
⑬
fence
g/s
Admergill Water
⑨ lane
Lanefield
lane
Lower wheathead
FB
⑦
⑧
⑭
⑮
Bank End is a very des. res.
Bank End
Blacko Foot
Blacko Water
⑯ WATER MEETINGS
FB
The line of beech trees was planted 300 years ago.
wall
Pendle Water
ancient oak
Old Oak Tree Cottage
weir
⑥
Hollin Farm Hall
Pendle Water
Inn
GP
wall
West Pasture
③
②
①
stepping stones
⑤
ROUGHLEE
high holly hedge
④
g/s
FB
lane
chimney
HIGHERFORD

60

A walk through typical PENDLE FOREST countryside - a blend of undulating meadowland, open moor and delightful riverside paths. From ROUGHLEE, a village notable for its 'witchly' associations, there is a long, steady climb to JACKSON'S HOUSE, a remote farm standing at over 1,000' on lonely BURN MOOR. Careful reference to map and directions is necessary to avoid going astray on this rather complex route. Dog-walkers should note that there are over 40 stiles along the way — some of them quite awkward. If PENDLE WATER is in full spate the stepping-stones (15 cylindrical concrete blocks) may not be crossable. Motor-road walking negligible.

SHORT CUT If you don't fancy the Burn Moor section follow the lane from point ⑨ to the bridge at point ⑭, thereby reducing the walk to 4 miles.

ROUTE DIRECTIONS *cont* : and continue downstream. ⑮► Turn R along lane. At farm take stile (PW sign) on L. Forward with wall, then fence, on L. ⑯► When fence ends keep straight on to stile and down to footbridge. Continue downstream. Cross big bridge and turn L (PW sign) along riverside path.

Roughlee
Old Hall

In the days when King Cotton ruled the region, ROUGHLEE was a popular Sunday afternoon venue for mill-workers out from the nearby grimy towns in search of some greenery and a breath of fresh air. Nowadays the crowds which flock to Roughlee are of a more heterogeneous nature, for the little village is a favourite haunt of walkers, cyclists, anglers, caravanners, campers and picnickers. The dominant building is the OLD HALL, a late-17th C. house now divided into cottages and much-altered, though still retaining some fine arch-headed mullion windows. Often referred to as 'WITCHES HALL', it is by repute the one-time home of ALICE NUTTER, one of the Pendle 'witches' who was hanged at Lancaster. It is more likely that she actually lived in a nearby, and now demolished, farmhouse. The severely eroded inscribed stone (THIS HOUSE WAS BUILDED BY MN IN THE YEAR OF OUR LORD 1536) set into the modernised west wing of the Hall originally belonged to the old farm. MN was Miles Nutter, whose son Richard was Alice's husband.

The *PACKHORSE BRIDGE* off Foreside, Higherford, dates from 1583. It is locally known as 'Owd Brig.'

★

WEST PASTURE and **LOWER WHEATHEAD** are 17th C. farmsteads. The latter displays the date 1606.

★

The huge OAK in the field near Old Oak Tree Cottage is estimated to be between 800 and 1,000 years old.

WATER MEETINGS
This was another popular picnic place for the mill-workers of bygone days.

MAP O.S. Explorer OL 21 South Pennines OR O.S. Explorer OL 41 Forest of Bowland and Ribblesdale.

A VISIT TO BRACEWELL

6½ MILES

22

P Gisburn. The village has no public car park. The best place to park is a small triangular roadside space (4-5 cars) at the extreme E end of the village. *Grid ref: 832 489* There are other small parking spaces by the toilets near the Auction Mart and alongside the A682 near the village centre.

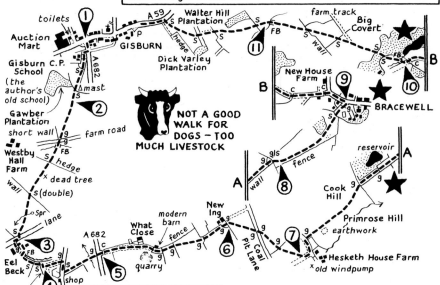

ROUTE DIRECTIONS

① From village centre go up A682. Turn R up school drive then L into narrow field. Straight on up to stile by mast. **②** Head directly for Pendle Hill through four fields via a line of gates and stiles. **③** Go R along lane and L into Eelbeck Farm drive. Take gate(wm) on L and cross footbridge behind house. Go L alongside stream through two stiles. **④** Turn R and follow FP signs into caravan park. Go L along main drive to exit at small gate by large gate blocked by boulders. Go R along lane and L over stile (wm). Straight up field to gate. **⑤** Cross A682 to follow farm road. Pass to R of modern barn. From second gate beyond barn go slightly R uphill to gate (wm) then forward to farm. **⑥** Go ½ R across field to gate. Cross lane to gate (FP sign). Bear R over shoulder of hill, through gate and slightly L uphill. **⑦** Go L along farm road. Just before reaching house fork L up rough track. Take gate (wm) on R and straight across big field to enter enclosed path to R of plantation. Follow wall to field corner. **⑧** ½ R up to fence and follow it forward. On approaching trees bear L to pass alongside fenced woodland. Drop to stile (wm) and keep L of tennis court to gate. **⑨** Go L along road then L along farm road. Keep straight on at fork to pass a reservoir. **⑩** 30yds past a cattle-grid take stile on R. Cross footbridge and bear slightly L up to stile and clear path through wood to stile at top. Maintain direction over hill and drop to wall-stile (50yds to L of farm track). Climb to top corner of field (stile) and drop to footbridge. **⑪** Head L,

cont. on next page

Lying amidst the soft emerald country-side at the far northern corner of the **BOROUGH OF PENDLE** is the hamlet of **BRACEWELL**. Though but a tiny cluster of farms and cottages, it is steeped in history and has one of the most beautiful churches in the area. This gently undulating walk is mostly through pathless pastures and should be avoided in late-Spring and early-Summer, when long grass can make progress slow and laborious. No ladder-stiles, and only ½ mile on motor-roads.

ROUTE DIRECTIONS cont : keeping below wood to reach its LH end. When Gisburn appears aim slightly to L of it, through two stiles, then bear R down sunken path to stile onto busy A59.

GISBURN is a quaint and charming village. Peaceful, however, it is not, for it is rent asunder by the constant stream of vehicles roaring and thundering along the A59. Crossing the main street unscathed requires agility and a modicum of luck, and next-of-kin should be informed before an attempt is made. The beautiful church has a 13th C. porch and 14th C. tower, and its lovely stained glass includes medieval fragments. The village retains some 17th C. cottages, and not so many years ago had four pubs. Now there is only one, the White Bull, named after the now extinct wild white cattle which long ago roamed in Gisburne Park.

Parish Church of St.Mary the Virgin, Gisburn

The GISBURN WITCH Jennet Preston was one of those arrested for being at the Good Friday 'witches' gathering at Malkin Tower. She was charged with causing the death,'by charms and sorcery,' of Thomas Lister of Westby Hall. As Gisburn was, in those days, in Yorkshire, she was sent for trial not to Lancaster but to York. Evidence was given that after Lister's death she was brought to the house and made to touch the body, which thereupon began to bleed. Only the touch of a murderer, it was stated, could cause a corpse to bleed. She was found guilty, and hanged on 29 July 1612 (three weeks before the Lancaster hangings).

RA·AA TA 16·14 IR

old doorhead, Gisburn

★

The **PRIMROSE HILL EARTHWORK**, a slightly raised area about 10yds square and barely discernible, is thought to mark the site of a Roman signal tower.

★

BRACEWELL church was originally a private chapel of the Tempest family. An archway from their manor house(demolished 1656) has been re-erected in the churchyard. A large nearby barn is known as 'King Henry's Parlour', for Henry VI is said to have taken refuge there as he fled from the Battle of Hexham.

MAP O.S. Explorer OL 21 South Pennines **OR** O.S. Explorer OL 41 Forest of Bowland and Ribblesdale.

PENDLE HILL
FROM DOWNHAM

6 MILES

P Downham. Car park and toilets at lower end of village, near the bridge.
Grid ref : 784 441

ROUTE DIRECTIONS

① From car park entrance go R (FP sign) up drive to gate/stile. Follow hedge on R past woodland on R to stile. **②** Straight on across field, passing far end of line of trees, to swing-gate/stile in corner. Follow fence on L and go down past a barn. **③** R along tarmac lane. When it turns R go straight on (SP Cul-de-sac) up a farm road. **④** At L bend of farm road go straight on up green path to stile at its end. **⑤** Go R to marker-post then climb steeply alongside ravine. At marker-stone bear R. Follow marker-stones across moor to wall and climb alongside it. **⑥** At wall-corner go ½ R to climb alongside prominent groove slanting up hillside. Eventually a cairned path swings L up to big memorial cairn. **⑦** Turn L (N) to follow path near escarpment on L. Cross a ladder-stile and follow broad path to gate/ladder-stile. Climb (s) to O.S. column at summit. **⑧** Return to gate/ladder-stile but don't cross it. Turn R to follow wall. **⑨** Cross wall at step-stile (GP Downham) to path leading directly away. It contours hillside before dropping to a marker-stone. Follow markers to zig-zag down to clear path passing to R of plantation. **⑩** Cross road to gate (FP Downham). Cross stile and go L to stile (wm) in front of a barn. Descend RH side of fields. **⑪** Cross farm road to wall-stile, follow fence down to a footbridge, then descend RH side of two fields. **⑫** In third field go ½ L, aiming towards a cluster of house chimneys. Walk alongside a stream to reach a stile into a lane at the bottom of the village. Feed the ducks and walk round Downham to expend any surplus energy.

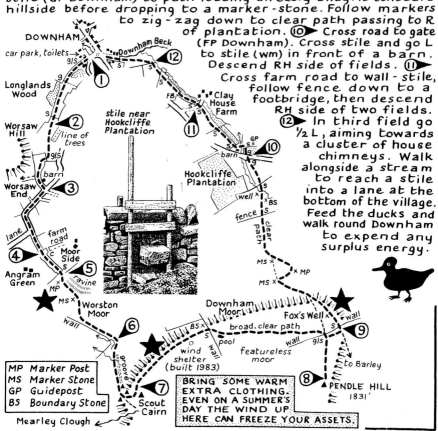

DOWNHAM
car park, toilets →
Downham Beck
Longlands Wood
Worsaw Hill
line of trees
stile near Hookcliffe Plantation
Clay House Farm
Worsaw End
barn
Hookcliffe Plantation
well
lane
farm road
Moor Side
Angram Green
ravine
Worston Moor
fence
clear path
Downham Moor
Fox's Well
to Barley
Wall
wind shelter (built 1983)
broad, clear path
pool
featureless moor
PENDLE HILL 1831'
Scout Cairn
Mearley Clough

MP Marker Post
MS Marker Stone
GP Guidepost
BS Boundary Stone

BRING SOME WARM EXTRA CLOTHING. EVEN ON A SUMMER'S DAY THE WIND UP HERE CAN FREEZE YOUR ASSETS.

64

One of the most beautiful, dramatic and exhilarating walks in the area. Generally easy walking, but with one strenuous section between points ⑤ and ⑦. This entails a climb - steep in places - of over 1000'. The low-level routes to and from the hill are through verdant pastures. On the hill the paths are mostly well-defined, with plenty of waymarks, but DON'T GO WITHOUT A COMPASS. Mist can descend suddenly on Pendle. 2 ladder-stiles. Motor-road walking negligible. Breathtaking views.

DOWNHAM is

undeniably the loveliest village in the Ribble Valley, if not in the whole of Lancashire.

Downham

Proudly and lovingly maintained, it has won many awards for its beauty and, despite being overrun by tourists and trippers, remains remarkably unspoiled and uncommercialised. DOWNHAM HALL, at the N end of the village, has been the family seat of the ASSHETONS (armorial shield shown above) since 1558. This Elizabethan mansion was extensively rebuilt in Georgian style in 1835. ST. LEONARD'S CHURCH was built as recently as 1910, though the tower has survived from a 15th C. church which was demolished in 1800. The late Queen Mary regarded the view from the porch as the most beautiful from any church porch in the land. At the lower end of the village, near the bridge, stands OLD WELL HALL, a superb Tudor house (see illustration P 44), and there are clusters of 18th and 19th C. HANDLOOM WEAVERS' COTTAGES. Children love to splash around in the pebbly stream, and corpulent mallard are equally happy gorging themselves on a never-ending supply of visitors' titbits. The highly acclaimed film 'WHISTLE DOWN THE WIND', starring Hayley Mills, was shot on location in the village and at Worsaw End in 1961.

WORSAW HILL

is a reef knoll — a smooth, rounded hillock of almost pure limestone. Some 300 million years ago, during the geological era known as the Carboniferous period, this area lay submerged beneath a shallow sea. Bodies of myriads of dead sea-creatures were swept by water currents into submarine ridges. In later geological times earth movements lifted these mounds of limestone above the level of the sea. Often they are quarried, but Worsaw Hill is safe, having been declared a Site of Special Scientific Interest (SSSI).

SCOUT CAIRN is a prominent Ribble Valley landmark, and 3 tablets built into the splendidly constructed monument explain its name. All the hard work is now behind you, and the walk from the cairn to the crosswall, along the rim of Pendle's northern escarpment, is the finest section of the route.

GEORGE FOX (1624-91), founder of the Quakers, climbed Pendle in

1652, found inspiration there and afterwards wrote, 'From the top of this hill the Lord let me see in what places He had a great people to be gathered. As I went down I found a spring of water in the side of the hill, with which I refreshed myself.' Look out for FOX'S WELL, which now has an iron lid.

MAP O.S. Explorer OL 21 South Pennines OR O.S. Explorer OL 41 Forest of Bowland and Ribblesdale.

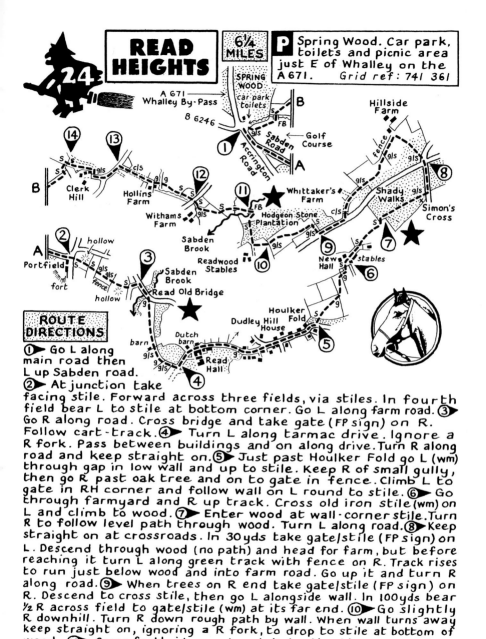

24 READ HEIGHTS

6¼ MILES

P Spring Wood. Car park, toilets and picnic area just E of Whalley on the A 671.   Grid ref: 741 361

Map labels: A 671 Whalley By-Pass · B 6246 · SPRING WOOD car park toilets · Accrington Road · Sabden Road · Golf Course · FB · Hillside Farm · fence · Whittaker's Farm · Shady Walks · Simon's Cross · Hodgeon Stone Plantation · Clerk Hill · Hollins Farm · Withams Farm · Sabden Brook · Readwood Stables · New Hall · stables · Portfield · fort · hollow · Sabden Brook · Read Old Bridge · Dudley Hill House · Houlker Fold · barn · Dutch barn · Read Hall

ROUTE DIRECTIONS

① Go L along main road then L up Sabden road. ② At junction take facing stile. Forward across three fields, via stiles. In fourth field bear L to stile at bottom corner. Go L along farm road. ③ Go R along road. Cross bridge and take gate (FP sign) on R. Follow cart-track. ④ Turn L along tarmac drive. Ignore a R fork. Pass between buildings and on along drive. Turn R along road and keep straight on. ⑤ Just past Houlker Fold go L (wm) through gap in low wall and up to stile. Keep R of small gully, then go R past oak tree and on to gate in fence. Climb L to gate in RH corner and follow wall on L round to stile. ⑥ Go through farmyard and R up track. Cross old iron stile (wm) on L and climb to wood. ⑦ Enter wood at wall-corner stile. Turn R to follow level path through wood. Turn L along road. ⑧ Keep straight on at crossroads. In 30 yds take gate/stile (FP sign) on L. Descend through wood (no path) and head for farm, but before reaching it turn L along green track with fence on R. Track rises to run just below wood and into farm road. Go up it and turn R along road. ⑨ When trees on R end take gate/stile (FP sign) on R. Descend to cross stile, then go L alongside wall. In 100 yds bear ½ R across field to gate/stile (wm) at its far end. ⑩ Go slightly R downhill. Turn R down rough path by wall. When wall turns away keep straight on, ignoring a R fork, to drop to stile at bottom of wood. ⑪ Cross footbridge and maintain direction across two fields to ladder-stile (wm). Follow powerline up to gate/stile (wm) then follow hedge round to stile. ⑫ Cross road and climb LH edge of field. In next field climb steeply (aim just R of farm) to gate (wm). Forward through small gate and out along farm road. ⑬ Go L along road. Fork R (FP sign) into drive. Just before gate into private grounds take gate/stile on R. Turn L to follow FIELD EDGE

cont. on next page

The lower SABDEN VALLEY is bounded on its south side by a low, wooded ridge known as READ HEIGHTS. The walk here described meanders through a region steeped in history and endowed with great scenic beauty. It is exceptionally lovely in late spring and early summer, when bluebells and rhododendrons adorn the woods and the hillsides blaze yellow with gorse. Lots of stiles, but only two ladder-stiles. I mile on motor-roads. Horses and horse muck all over the place.

ROUTE DIRECTIONS cont.: (NOT cart-track). ⑭ Cross fence – stile (wm) then L over another and L again over another. Turn R to descend alongside fence. When it turns away go L across to slab bridge then down edge of golf course.

SPRING WOOD

is hugely popular with picnickers and dog-walkers. A labyrinth of paths wind through beautiful woodland of birch, beech and Scots pine, and in May the bluebells make a superb show. Squirrels abound, and in winter visitors will sometimes see flocks of long-tailed tits.

READ OLD BRIDGE

was the site of a Civil War skirmish in April 1643. Here an army of Lancashire Royalists (Cavaliers) was ambushed and routed by a small band of local Parliamentarians (Roundheads).

Read Hall

Nowell nup. Dns. de Read

features prominently in the saga of the Pendle Witches, for it was the home of ROGER NOWELL J.P., the squire/magistrate who was responsible for bringing the 'witches' to trial in 1612. The Nowell estate was sold in 1772 to the Fort family, who built the present Regency-style mansion between 1818 and 1835.

SHADY WALKS AND SIMON'S CROSS

The overgrown trench alongside the path in SHADY WALKS was a drift mine for the extraction of fire clay. The old base of SIMON'S CROSS, which marked the boundary separating Read and Simonstone, is locally known as 'WART WELL', for the water which collects in its socket is said to cure warts.

Simon's Cross

footbridge, Sabden Brook

MAP O.S. Explorer 19 West Pennine Moors.

For notes on CLERK HILL see WALK 20

WHITE MOOR & ADMERGILL WATER

7¼ MILES   **P** Blacko Foot. ¼ mile from Blacko along the A682 Gisburn road turn L down lane (SP Roughlee 1¼). Small layby at bottom of hill by bridge.   Grid ref: 850 415

ROUTE DIRECTIONS

①► Walk L up lane. **②►** Go R along main road to gate/stile (FP sign) on L. Head R, climbing slightly, to stile in crosswall. Pass L of house and straight on, with wall on R. **③►** Just past bend in wall take stile (wm). Cross field to stile. Forward along farm road. **④►** Pass R of all buildings and on through stiles to pass R of next farm. Continue through stiles, heading towards chimneys of next house. **⑤►** Cross fence-stile into garden. Cross lawn to its LH corner, through pergola to stile, then forward to locate wall-stile on L. Head out along drive. When it bends L keep straight on through gates and along road. Straight on at junction. **⑥►** At post box turn L onto a rough lane and immediately L again. Keep L at fork. Through small gate and follow path straight on to chapel. Cross footbridge and forward with fence on R. **⑦►** Pass R of farm and bear L to stile. Go R up road. **⑧►** At Fanny Grey Inn turn L (FP Gisburn Old Road) up rough track. Beyond farm continue between walls up to gate/stile. **⑨►** Bear R to gate on skyline. Continue along cart-track. Turn L along walled track. **⑩►** Take stile by metal gate on R. Head L (towards Pendle) to gate in wall, then another gate at wall-corner. Follow wall cont. below R

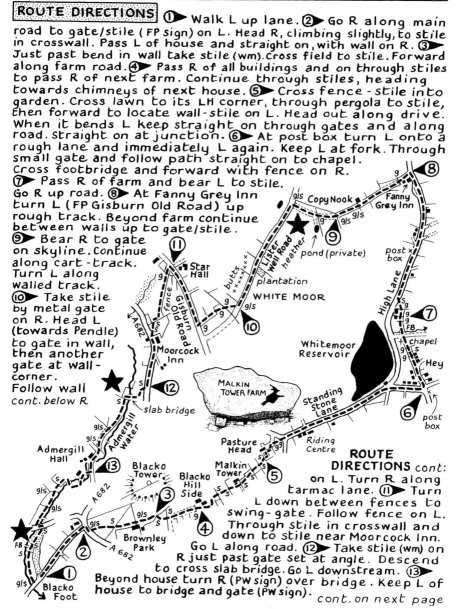

ROUTE DIRECTIONS cont: on L. Turn R along tarmac lane. **⑪►** Turn L down between fences to swing-gate. Follow fence on L. Through stile in crosswall and down to stile near Moorcock Inn. Go L along road. **⑫►** Take stile (wm) on R just past gate set at angle. Descend to cross slab bridge. Go L downstream. **⑬►** Beyond house turn R (PW sign) over bridge. Keep L of house to bridge and gate (PW sign).   cont. on next page

68

This stimulating walk, on the fringe of PENDLE FOREST, reaches a height of just over 1100' without involving any steep climbing. The route encircles BLACKO TOWER, one of the area's best-known landmarks. The terrain is delightfully varied, with rolling pastures giving way to bleak moorland and, finally, the delectable little valley of ADMERGILL WATER. Two excellent pubs en route. No ladder-stiles. Just under 2 miles on motor-roads which can be busy at weekends. A complex route; follow directions carefully.

ROUTE DIRECTIONS cont:

Follow stream, crossing to its RH side at footbridge. At road bridge go L to stile and follow path on LH side of stream. Ignore footbridge.

BLACKO TOWER or *Stansfield Tower*, or *Jonathan's Folly*, was built by Jonathan Stansfield, a local grocer, in 1890. It was restored in 1950.

MALKIN TOWER FARM is believed by some historians to stand near the site of MALKIN TOWER, the home of the DEMDIKE brood. Behind the farmhouse a short, high section of ancient wall set into a lower wall may have been part of the witches' hovel, but this is only conjecture. (see Walk 9). The wall is on private land, but can be seen in retrospect from the approach to Pasture Head. Parts of the present farmhouse date from c1700.

MOUNT PLEASANT METHODIST CHAPEL (near point 7) was converted from a pair of cottages and opened in 1822. A steep flight of outside steps leads up to the tiny first-floor chapel. The nearby stream (County Brook) used to be the Yorks/Lancs boundary.

The **FANNY GREY INN** was built around 1914 on the site of a much older building which was probably a farm that took to catering for passing travellers. There are various vague explanations as to how the pub came by its unusual name — mostly involving a racehorse and a long-gone landlady.

NOTE: There is no RIGHT-OF-WAY up to Blacko Tower. Permission to visit must be sought at Tower Farm, reached from the A682 half-a-mile north of point 2.

GISBURN OLD ROAD was the main route for packhorses to Gisburn until a turnpike road (now the A682) was built.

Moorcock Inn

ADMERGILL HALL, A SPLENDID EARLY 17TH C. BUILDING, STANDS BY AN OLD COLNE-WHALLEY PACKHORSE ROUTE. NOTE NEARBY THE OLD SLAB BRIDGE. OVER THE CENTURIES A DEEP GROOVE HAS BEEN WORN ALONG IT BY THE PASSAGE OF COUNTLESS FEET AND HOOVES.

MAP O.S. Explorer OL 21 South Pennines **OR** O.S. Explorer OL 41 Forest of Bowland and Ribblesdale.

WHALLEY & THE NAB

5¾ MILES

P Whalley. Car park at village centre, between Whalley Arms and Medical Centre. *Grid ref : 734 362*
Note : Car park is Pay and Display, but customers of Whalley Arms may reclaim parking fee.

ROUTE DIRECTIONS

①▶ From car park cross main street and pass L of Dog Inn to church. From far end of churchyard continue through The Square to the abbey. Return to main street and turn R. ②▶ Cross bridge and go L up Moor Lane. ③▶ At first bend turn L (BW sign) up track with wall on L. At a seat the path divides. Footpath on L is drier underfoot than bridleway on R. When paths re-unite keep close to wall on L, and at top of climb keep straight ahead. ④▶ At White Goat Farm keep L (FP Great Harwood) along rough track. Ignore a path forking L to a stile. ⑤▶ Just before reaching next farm cross farm road and bear R along enclosed green track. ⑥▶ At Scout Camp go R up tarmac lane. ⑦▶ 100 yds after passing end of road to Cowden take stile on L (FP sign). Forward with wall on L to pass through woodland. ⑧▶ Turn R along road. Straight on at crossroads. ⑨▶ Turn R down Goldacre Lane. At foot of hill fork L to follow track to reservoir. Walk along top of dam. ⑩▶ Go through facing gate at its far end, then turn R and follow fence to a pipe in a hollow. Go up past pipe and turn R to follow wall. Keep above trees to follow clear path through gorse. ⑪▶ Path swings L alongside old cart track, and joins it just past a gate. When wall on R turns away keep straight on to stile (wm) at far RH corner of field. Cross field to stile into wood. ⑫▶ Bear R through wood to stile. Continue along path through younger trees to reach tarmac lane, along which go R. ⑬▶ Go L at T-junction. ⑭▶ Fork R (FP sign) up drive of Wood Nook. Pass R of house to stile and forward alongside embankment. When it ends bear ½ R towards tall trees. ⑮▶ At fence turn L and descend to stile. Cross farm road to another stile and descend by fence on L to rejoin outward route.

Whalley Arches (viaduct)
WHALLEY
The Square
River Calder
Abbey ①
car toilets park
Whalley Bridge
weir
②
Bridge Cottage
③
⑭
Nab Wood
THE NAB ⑮
TV mast
Whalley Banks Farm
④
⑬
Moor Lane
Miles Hill
barn
⑤
tarmac
Heys Farm
⑫
rubble
wall
⑪
Dean Brook
Sunny Bank
Dean Bridge
Dean Wood
Bowley Scout Camp
broken walls
gorse
ignore stile here
Hawthorn and Rose Cottages
⑥
Dean Cottage
pipe
ruin
⑩
Bowley Hill
⑦
Cowden
⑧
Dean Clough Reservoir
⑨
Great Harwood Cricket Club (Ribblesdale League)

WHALLEY is renowned for its Abbey and quite superb Parish Church. WHALLEY AND THE NAB' is a convenient title, but the walk extends well to the south of THE NAB, crossing the pleasantly wooded DEAN VALLEY to reach the outskirts of GREAT HARWOOD. There are fine views, particularly of PENDLE HILL and across to the BOWLAND FELLS. Parts of the bridleway between points ③ and ⑤ can be very slutchy in wet weather. No ladder-stiles. 1¼ miles on mostly quiet motor-roads. Go here in May when DEAN WOOD has a carpet of bluebells and SUNNY BANK is ablaze with gorse.

Whalley Parish Church

This large village has sufficient charm and historical interest to attract thousands of visitors a year. THE SQUARE is the old village centre, and most of its buildings date from the 17th C., but in addition to these Whalley has many lovely old cottages and fine Tudor and Georgian houses.

WHALLEY
Twinned with
VIHIERS
FRANCE

But Whalley's pride and joy is undoubtedly THE PARISH CHURCH OF ST. MARY AND ALL SAINTS — once the Mother Church for half of Lancashire. An excellent guidebook is available, and its pages are crammed with information on the wealth of treasures to be seen in and around a truly outstanding church with a history spanning thirteen centuries.

In 1288 a small company of Cistercian monks came to Whalley from Stanlow Abbey in Cheshire to found a new monastery. They met with many difficulties, and it was not until 1308 that the foundation stone was laid. The early parts of the Abbey were built of golden-brown gritstone quarried on Whalley Nab. The Abbey took 127 years to build and became one of the most powerful in the North of England. There are two very fine gateways; the West Gate is backed rather incongruously by the red-brick railway viaduct known as 'Whalley Arches', which was officially opened 20 June 1850. The structure is 697yds long and has 49 arches, the central ones being 40' high. The West Gate is the oldest part of the Abbey (early 14th C.) and the room above the arch was a chapel for guests. Note the arch's superb rib-vaulting. The Abbey is open daily from 10am to 5pm, and has a coffee shop, gift shop and exhibition centre.

The Abbey
N.E. Gate

The heraldic shields in Whalley Church's unusual and beautiful east window include the arms of several local families who were involved in the 'Witch Trials' of 1612.

Assheton
Dns. de Downham

Banastre
Dns. de Altham

Nowell
nup. Dns. de Read

Holden
de Holden

BRIDGE COTTAGE, near Whalley Bridge, is where Harrison Ainsworth wrote his famous novel 'The Lancashire Witches' (1848).

MAP O.S. Explorer 19 West Pennine Moors.

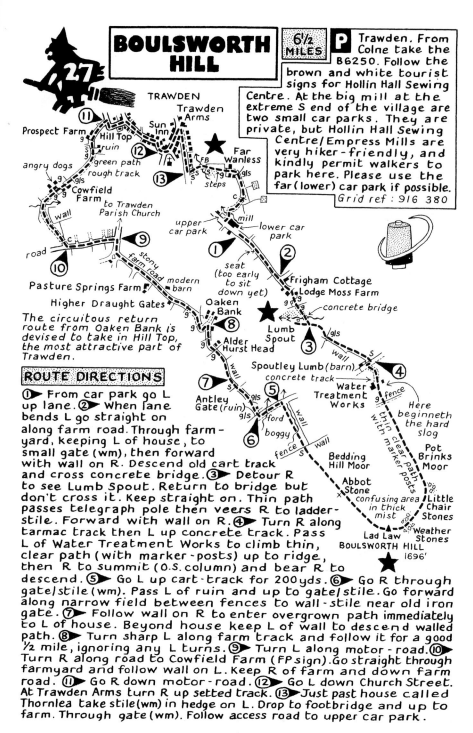

BOULSWORTH HILL

6½ MILES

P Trawden. From Colne take the B6250. Follow the brown and white tourist signs for Hollin Hall Sewing Centre. At the big mill at the extreme S end of the village are two small car parks. They are private, but Hollin Hall Sewing Centre/Empress Mills are very hiker-friendly, and kindly permit walkers to park here. Please use the far (lower) car park if possible.

Grid ref : 916 380

TRAWDEN
Trawden Arms
Sun Inn
Prospect Farm
Hill Top
ruin
green path
rough track
angry dogs
Cowfield Farm
to Trawden Parish Church
wall
road
Pasture Springs Farm
Higher Draught Gates
modern barn
FB
Far Wanless
steps
upper car park
mill
lower car park
seat (too early to sit down yet)
Frigham Cottage
Lodge Moss Farm
concrete bridge
Oaken Bank
Lumb Spout
Alder Hurst Head
Spoutley Lumb (barn)
concrete track
Water Treatment Works
Antley Gate (ruin)
ford
boggy
fence
wall
Bedding Hill Moor
Abbot Stone
Here beginneth the hard slog
Pot Brinks Moor
confusing area in thick mist
Little Chair Stones
Weather Stones
Lad Law
BOULSWORTH HILL
1696'
thin clear path with marker posts

The circuitous return route from Oaken Bank is devised to take in Hill Top, the most attractive part of Trawden.

ROUTE DIRECTIONS

① From car park go L up lane. ② When lane bends L go straight on along farm road. Through farm-yard, keeping L of house, to small gate (wm), then forward with wall on R. Descend old cart track and cross concrete bridge. ③ Detour R to see Lumb Spout. Return to bridge but don't cross it. Keep straight on. Thin path passes telegraph pole then veers R to ladder-stile. Forward with wall on R. ④ Turn R along tarmac track then L up concrete track. Pass L of Water Treatment Works to climb thin, clear path (with marker-posts) up to ridge, then R to summit (O.S. column) and bear R to descend. ⑤ Go L up cart-track for 200yds. ⑥ Go R through gate/stile (wm). Pass L of ruin and up to gate/stile. Go forward along narrow field between fences to wall-stile near old iron gate. ⑦ Follow wall on R to enter overgrown path immediately to L of house. Beyond house keep L of wall to descend walled path. ⑧ Turn sharp L along farm track and follow it for a good ½ mile, ignoring any L turns. ⑨ Turn L along motor-road. ⑩ Turn R along road to Cowfield Farm (FP sign). Go straight through farmyard and follow wall on L. Keep R of farm and down farm road. ⑪ Go R down motor-road. ⑫ Go L down Church Street. At Trawden Arms turn R up setted track. ⑬ Just past house called Thornlea take stile (wm) in hedge on L. Drop to footbridge and up to farm. Through gate (wm). Follow access road to upper car park.

A strenuous walk for which clear weather is essential. The North West Water Authority's steep concessionary path allows access to the top of BOULSWORTH. Some boggy patches will be encountered on the moor. The final 2¾ miles, from OAKEN BANK, is mostly on roads and farm tracks. 2 ladder-stiles (one with adjacent gate). ¾ mile on quiet motor-roads. IT'S A WASTE OF EFFORT TO CLIMB BOULSWORTH IN MIST. IF, ON ARRIVING AT POINT 4, YOU CAN'T SEE THE HILL, FORGET IT AND FOLLOW THE TRACK DIRECTLY TO POINT 5.

TRAWDEN

TRAWDEN was a small, ancient settlement which expanded enormously during the reign of 'King Cotton'. The **HILL TOP** area, the oldest part of the village, is a delightfully haphazard jumble of 17th and 18th century buildings. The unprepossessing **PARISH CHURCH** was built 1845-6. Trawden's two pubs are as different as chalk and cheese. The **SUN INN**, a hostelry of immense character, dates back to the 18th C.; the late-Victorian **TRAWDEN ARMS** (until recently called the Rock Inn) was built in 1895 on the site of an old corn mill. The setted **TRAMWAY** running up from the Trawden Arms was opened 21-12-1905 to allow trams to bypass the main street which, beyond the Rock, was too narrow for them to negotiate. The last tram left Trawden 3-6-1928.

A Trawden tram of the 1920s

LITTLE MOSS — unusual sign near point 9

BOULSWORTH'S summit ridge, with its groups of bizarre gritstone outcrops, is a grand place to be on the right kind of day. The actual summit is called 'Lad Law', and an altar-shaped stone near the O.S. column is thought to have been used by Druids for sacrificial offerings.

LUMB SPOUT

is a slender waterfall set in a lovely wooded hollow. In its heyday as a beauty spot there was a cafe here – the ruins can be seen just above the waterfall.

OAKEN BANK is a tiny hamlet, but there was a time when more than 100 people – many of them handloom weavers – lived here.

One of the Airstead herd of pedigree friesians based at the aptly named Cowfield Farm.

FAR WANLESS is an attractive early 17th C. house. The datestone (1753) above the door came from elsewhere, and, in the owner's opinion, was probably placed here within the last 100 years. Prior to the Toleration Act of 1689 Far Wanless was secretly used as a Friends' Meeting House.

On completion of the walk award yourself a delicious afternoon tea, complete with scone, jam & cream, at BOBBINS CAFE.

MAP   O.S. Explorer OL 21 South Pennines.   DOGS ON LEADS ON BOULSWORTH PLEASE

73

KELBROOK MOOR

28

7 MILES

P Kelbrook. From church take lane which starts between stream (on L) and long barn. 170yds along it, on L by stone bridge, is a layby. Grid ref: 904 446

ROUTE DIRECTIONS

① Walk along lane with stream on L. Just past Dotcliffe Mill lane bends L. ② Take stile on R (wm Kelbrook Circular Walk). Climb to stile but DON'T USE IT. Turn L (wm) and follow line of trees to stile. Turn R and climb through 3 fields. Go L along farm road. ③ Straight through farmyard to stile. Forward with fence on R and on to gate/stile. Head for house. Pass L of it along gravel path to gate. Cross footbridge to path slanting R up hillside. ④ Pass L of house to join farm road. When it turns L go R to wall-stile. Head L across rough field then climb alongside wall on L. ⑤ At rear of pub take gate/stile (PW sign) on L. Turn L along road then R along Warley Wise Lane. ⑥ Turn R (PW sign) along farm road. Follow it round a small plantation. ⑦ When farm road turns L towards farm keep straight on alongside fence/wall. Cross stile by O.S. column and follow wall on L to stile. Head for farm. Enter yard at stile, pass R of buildings and out along farm road. ⑧ When it bends L go straight forward to gate/stile (PW sign). Follow track by wall on R. At house take gate/stile on R. Path goes straight ahead through gates then bears R to next farm. Go L along farm road. ⑨ Turn L down road then R up farm road to Harwes Farm. Go L along enclosed track. ⑩ Take ladder-stile on R and cross moor. Keep just R of trees then descend L (aim to R of small lake) to gate/stile

cont. on next page

SHORT CUT If you're a bit weary, or pushed for time (having spent too long in the Hare and Hounds), you could turn R at point ⑤ and proceed by road to point ⑨ (½ mile). The walk would then be reduced to 5 miles.

74

This invigorating WEST CRAVEN ramble provides outstanding views from a succession of splendid vantage points. It's a grand place to be — especially in spring, when the upland pastures resound with the exultant song of the skylark and the wild, haunting call of the curlew. In late summer, too, the walk is a joy, for then the moors are ablaze with heather. Undulating, with some rough moorland walking (good footwear essential). 4 ladder-stiles (2 with adjacent gates). 1¼ miles on quiet motor-roads. Excellent refreshments at the Hare and Hounds.

ROUTE DIRECTIONS cont : in wall. ⑪ Follow wall on L. When it starts to descend towards farm keep straight on (wm on wall), maintaining height, to ladder-stile. Straight down field to stile, then down tarmac lane. ⑫ Turn R at bottom of Cob Lane and R again at bridge.

KELBROOK

Scald Bank

Though Kelbrook is recorded as a 'township' (Chelbroc) in the Domesday Book, it was not until the early 19th C., when a wool-spinning water-mill was built, that it began to grow into a sizeable community. When power looms were introduced the mill produced both cotton and wool cloth, but textile manufacture ceased when the mill was severely fire-damaged in 1959. St. Mary's Church was consecrated as a chapel-of-ease (for Thornton -in-Craven) in 1839. The tower has, unusually, a clock-face on all its four sides. Kelbrook is a spick-and-span village which gives the impression that its residents really care about it. There are some lovely old houses and, facing each other across the main road, a good pub and a first-class 'chippy'.

BLACK LANE ENDS

IN BYGONE DAYS THERE WAS A PUB, A METHODIST CHAPEL AND A SCHOOL HERE. ONLY THE PUB — THE **HARE AND HOUNDS** — IS STILL IN BUSINESS. THIS FRIENDLY AND COSY HOSTELRY SELLS TIMOTHY TAYLOR'S ALE, THE FINEST IN THE NORTH (IN THE AUTHOR'S OPINION).

TOM CROSS

This carved stone set in a wall near Harwes Farm marks the spot where nonconformists held religious meetings in the days when they were forbidden to worship within five miles of any established church.

Knarrs Hill

Cloudberry

KELBROOK MOOR is at its loveliest when the heather's in bloom, but many other moorland plants, such as cotton-grass, bilberry and sphagnum moss thrive here. Cloudberry, a quite rare plant, may occasionally be seen. The O.S. column on SHEEP HILL, the highest point of the moor, is in view away to your R (no right-of-way).

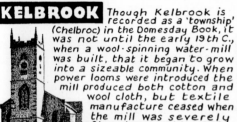

MAP	O.S. Explorer OL 21 South Pennines.

AROUND STANG TOP

29

4¾ MILES

P Barley. Car park, toilets and small info. centre/shop at S end of village.

Grid ref: 823 403

ROUTE DIRECTIONS

① At far (E) end of car park a path (wm) leads out onto a tarmac lane. Go L along it, pass between cottages of Narrowgates and along streamside track. ② On reaching PW sign on R, turn L (Holly House on your L). Follow road through hamlet and uphill to R. ③ Take stile by small red-brick building to follow woodland path. On reaching a stile at far edge of wood DON'T CROSS IT, but go L (permissive path). ④ From next stile go L up steps, then bear R to another stile. Follow conifers on R to stile (PW sign), descend to drive and go L along it. ⑤ Go L up lane and R along Hollin Top farm road. ⑥ On reaching PW sign on R, turn L and climb hillside to gate by holly bush. Follow broad path, curving L around hillside. ⑦ When track forks keep R down to stile onto farm track. Just before farm turn L (FP sign) uphill to to take gate/stile on R. Descend RH side of field to gate/stile by tiny stream. ⑧ Climb with wall on R. Immediately past farm take gate/stile and continue along RH side of wall. ⑨ Turn L along road. In 60yds take stile on R and go ½ L to cross another stile. Turn R and follow field boundary to farm. ⑩ Use a gate/stile on R to pass round to R of all buildings. Continue forward down to gate just L of derelict farm. Cross tiny stream and head L towards small stand of conifers. Join wall coming in from R. ⑪ Go R along road. ⑫ Go L through gate (FP sign). A clear path drops through gate in crosswall and eventually becomes a walled lane. ⑬ Just before reaching reservoir take small gate (wm) on R. Follow reservoir wall, via two swing-gates, and descend to Over Houses. ⑭ Cross bridge and take small gate (wm) on R to follow streamside path. ⑮ Turn R along lane then L through the village.

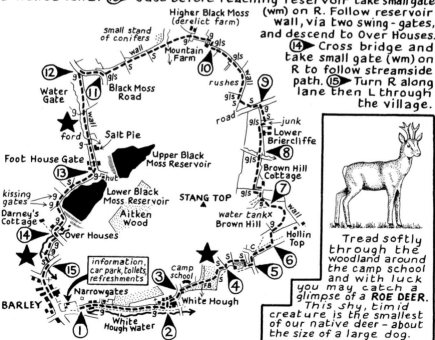

Higher Black Moss (derelict farm)

small stand of conifers

wall

Mountain Farm

Water Gate ⑫

Black Moss Road

⑪

rushes

⑩

⑨

road

junk

Lower Briercliffe

⑧

Brown Hill Cottage

⑦

STANG TOP

water tank×
Brown Hill

Hollin Top

⑥

⑤

Foot House Gate

ford

Salt Pie

Upper Black Moss Reservoir

⑬

hut

Lower Black Moss Reservoir

Aitken Wood

kissing gates

Darney's Cottage

⑭

Over Houses

⑮

information, car park, toilets refreshments

③

camp school

④

BARLEY

Narrowgates

White Hough

White Hough Water

①

②

Tread softly through the woodland around the camp school and with luck you may catch a glimpse of a **ROE DEER**. This shy, timid creature is the smallest of our native deer — about the size of a large dog.

STANG TOP MOOR is one of Pendle's eastern foothills. The walk begins in sylvan surroundings, following a sparkling stream down its wooded valley from BARLEY to WHITE HOUGH, before heading north to encounter a much more open and bleak landscape. Some interesting old buildings are seen on this short, easy ramble over gently undulating terrain. In wet weather some of the fields may be glutinous, particularly in the vicinity of LOWER BRIERCLIFFE. No ladder-stiles, but dog-walkers may find some of the wall-stiles a bit awkward. ¼ mile on motor-roads.

BARLEY

The Barley Mow Restaurant

This small, attractive village is highly popular with ramblers and tourists. It began life as a 13th C vaccary, and was called 'Barelegh' (infertile lea or meadow). The imposing Pendle Inn was built in 1930.

The isolated chimney at NARROWGATES belonged to a water-powered cotton-mill. On closing down in 1967 the oldest parts were demolished and the rest converted into a private house. The mill-pond was filled in to create the visitors' car park. The two attractive rows of weavers' cottages were restored in the 1970s.

★

WHITE HOUGH has a long history, for it is known that a vaccary (cattle farm) existed here in the 13th C. The Grange has, on its porch, the inscription 'THIS HOUS WAS BUILDED BY CHRISTOFER BULLCOCKE AND JENET HIS WYFE 1593'.

★

The CAMP SCHOOL was founded in 1939 to give children from industrial towns the opportunity to enjoy the countryside.

Higher Black Moss Farm

UPPER BLACK MOSS RESERVOIR. Built: 1894. Area : 12¾ acres. Max Depth : 31'. Capacity : 45 million gallons.
LOWER BLACK MOSS RESERVOIR. Built: 1903 . Area : 17¾ acres. Max Depth : 41'. Capacity : 65 million gallons.

Both reservoirs supply drinking water to Nelson.

THE HOUSE WITH THE CURIOUS NAME OF SALT PIE STANDS BY AN ANCIENT CARTERS' TRACK BETWEEN DOWNHAM AND GOLDSHAW BOOTH. THE NAME COMES FROM THE PILE (PIE) OF SALT THAT USED TO BE STORED HERE FOR SALE AS A FOOD PRESERVATIVE.

cottage at Over Houses

Darney's Cottage

Built c1580. William Darney, a cobbler and preacher, came south with Bonny Prince Charlie, and lived here from 1746 to his death in 1774. The house can be reached via a gate/stile to the L of the white house at Over Houses. The illustration shows how the house looked in 1991. It is now being restored.

MAP O.S. Explorer OL 21 South Pennines OR O.S. Explorer OL 41 Forest of Bowland and Ribblesdale.

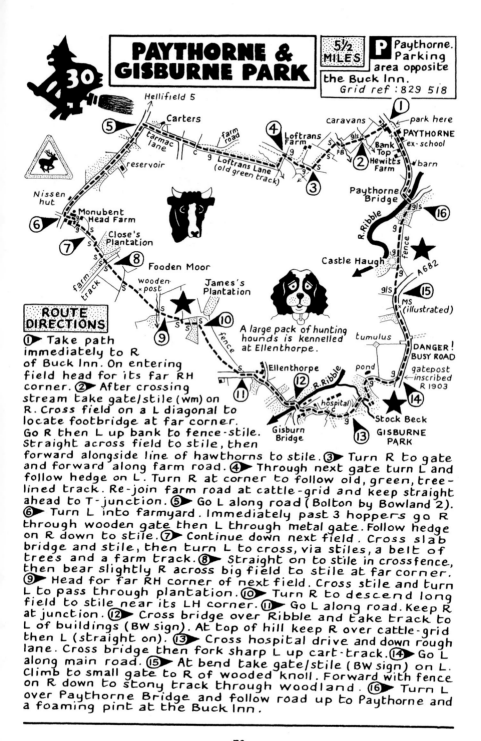

PAYTHORNE & GISBURNE PARK

5½ MILES

P Paythorne. Parking area opposite the Buck Inn.
Grid ref: 829 518

Map labels:

Hellifield 5 · Carters · tarmac lane · farm road · reservoir · Loftrans Farm · Loftrans Lane (old green track) · caravans · park here · PAYTHORNE · ex-school · Bank Top · Hewitts Farm · barn · Paythorne Bridge · R. Ribble · fence · A682 · Castle Haugh · Nissen hut · Monubent Head Farm · Close's Plantation · Fooden Moor · wooden post · James's Plantation · MS (illustrated) · DANGER! BUSY ROAD · gatepost ←inscribed R 1903 · A large pack of hunting hounds is kennelled at Ellenthorpe. · tumulus · Ellenthorpe · pond · R. Ribble · hospital · Stock Beck · Gisburn Bridge · GISBURNE PARK · farm track

ROUTE DIRECTIONS

① Take path immediately to R of Buck Inn. On entering field head for its far RH corner. ② After crossing stream take gate/stile (wm) on R. Cross field on a L diagonal to locate footbridge at far corner. Go R then L up bank to fence-stile. Straight across field to stile, then forward alongside line of hawthorns to stile. ③ Turn R to gate and forward along farm road. ④ Through next gate turn L and follow hedge on L. Turn R at corner to follow old, green, tree-lined track. Re-join farm road at cattle-grid and keep straight ahead to T-junction. ⑤ Go L along road (Bolton by Bowland 2). ⑥ Turn L into farmyard. Immediately past 3 hoppers go R through wooden gate then L through metal gate. Follow hedge on R down to stile. ⑦ Continue down next field. Cross slab bridge and stile, then turn L to cross, via stiles, a belt of trees and a farm track. ⑧ Straight on to stile in crossfence, then bear slightly R across big field to stile at far corner. ⑨ Head for far RH corner of next field. Cross stile and turn L to pass through plantation. ⑩ Turn R to descend long field to stile near its LH corner. ⑪ Go L along road. Keep R at junction. ⑫ Cross bridge over Ribble and take track to L of buildings (BW sign). At top of hill keep R over cattle-grid then L (straight on). ⑬ Cross hospital drive and down rough lane. Cross bridge then fork sharp L up cart-track. ⑭ Go L along main road. ⑮ At bend take gate/stile (BW sign) on L. Climb to small gate to R of wooded knoll. Forward with fence on R down to stony track through woodland. ⑯ Turn L over Paythorne Bridge and follow road up to Paythorne and a foaming pint at the Buck Inn.

A leisurely stroll in that beautiful part of CRAVEN where the RIBBLE swings westwards into LANCASHIRE. Easy walking, but can be very muddy after rain. Plenty of stiles — nearly all of them waymarked — but no ladder-stiles. 1½ miles on motor-roads. This is all lovely countryside — lush, peaceful and pastoral — and on a sunny autumn day the section between GISBURN BRIDGE and STOCK BECK is an extravagant riot of colour.

DANGER **TAKE EXTREME CARE** on the ⅓ mile section of the A682 between points ⑮ and ⑯. This is a very busy road, with a constant stream of huge quarry lorries travelling far too fast.

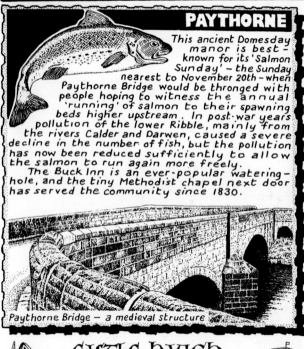

PAYTHORNE

This ancient Domesday manor is best-known for its 'Salmon Sunday' – the Sunday nearest to November 20th – when Paythorne Bridge would be thronged with people hoping to witness the annual 'running' of salmon to their spawning beds higher upstream. In post-war years pollution of the lower Ribble, mainly from the rivers Calder and Darwen, caused a severe decline in the number of fish, but the pollution has now been reduced sufficiently to allow the salmon to run again more freely.

The Buck Inn is an ever-popular watering-hole, and the tiny Methodist chapel next door has served the community since 1830.

Paythorne Bridge — a medieval structure

GISBURNE PARK HALL

IS GLORIOUSLY SITED ON AN EMINENCE OVERLOOKING THE CONFLUENCE OF THE RIBBLE AND STOCK BECK. THE ELEGANT FAÇADE IS GEORGIAN, DATING FROM 1750, BUT THE HALL IS OLDER THAN THAT AND WAS ORIGINALLY CALLED LOWER HALL. THE LISTERS, WHOSE FAMILY SEAT THIS WAS, WERE LORDS OF RIBBLESDALE, WITH VAST ESTATES STRETCHING FROM CLITHEROE TO MALHAM. THE HALL IS NOW A PRIVATE HOSPITAL, AND ITS DRIVE PASSES THROUGH RICHLY WOODED PARKLAND WHERE WILD WHITE CATTLE USED TO ROAM.
'Gisburne' is the old spelling – the village dropped the 'e' more than a century ago.

CASTLE HAUGH

This huge, 25' high wooded mound, encircled by a dry, 7' deep ditch, is almost certainly the site of an early Norman motte and bailey castle. On top of the motte (hill) would have stood a wooden keep. The motte drops steeply to the river on its west side, and the bailey (fenced enclosure) would have been extremely difficult to capture.

To Settle 10 Miles

MAP O.S. Explorer OL41 Forest of Bowland and Ribblesdale.

NOTES

From ghoulies and ghosties and long leggety beasties,
And things that go bump in the night,
Good Lord deliver us.
Amen